I Am
Glad

Journey to Faith

Gladys McCay Russell

I Am Glad
Journey to Faith
by Gladys McCay Russell

Printed in the United States of America.

ISBN 9781498436885

www.xulonpress.com

Grandma Gladys takes her beloved
Grandchildren through lessons learned on her
journey to faith.

Table of Contents

Blest Beginnings

The momentous occasions had arrived. After surviving a humid, bug infested summer on the little North Dakota farm, it was time to bring another McCay into the world. A month overdue with child, my poor mother could hardly wait to be delivered. Thankfully, she and dad were living in a tiny farmhouse with dad's parents, Grandma and Grandpa McCay. They could take care of big brother Eddie, fast approaching, age 2, while dad fired up the old model A and took his young wife, already in labor, off to have a genuine doctor delivered baby.

Mercifully, the weather seemed clear because they would have to drive over 30 miles of precarious roads and over the state line to McIntosh South Dakota to locate the nearest doctor. They were thankful to have heard there was a doctor even this close. In 1938, doctors were scarce in this part of the Dakota plains and they already blamed themselves for the lack of care a good doctor might have provided when they lost their first baby, Kenneth Roger McCay at only 6 weeks old.

There were no phones to notify the doctor that they were coming, and there was no way of letting anyone know if they had car trouble and didn't make it. Luckily, the dirt roads had hardened after a long summer, but an unexpected thunderstorm could change that at any time. The roads were bumpy from all the ruts that had occurred from previous storms. It was a rough ride for anyone—let alone a young lady already feeling the pangs of childbirth.

Arriving in McIntosh, they were able to rent a room in a boarding house while dad located the doctor who was supposed to be there. Unfortunately, the doctor was nowhere to be found. It turns out he was a fraud and had been run out of town. A mid-wife was quickly located and despite unsettling beginnings, I came into the world with gusto and at a whopping 10-pounds the battle with weight was off to a good start.

It didn't take mom long to notice that the boarding house was infested with bedbugs and she would have none of that. She demanded that dad pack us both up and go home immediately (mom was always a fastidious housekeeper even in the most trying of circumstances.)

If you could have seen the little North Dakota farm that welcomed me toward the end of the Great Depression, I am sure you would have been appalled at our living conditions; maybe, you would be a little sorry for poor Grandma Gladys. The Old McCay Farm wasn't quite as cozy as the farms pictured in those Old McDonald books, but it was a wonderful place to put down roots and to develop an appreciation for the nicer things that would come later.

Our farm was located on property that had originally been homesteaded by my Grandpa McCay. There were few trees with exception of those borderingand nourished by occasional creeks. The land in Southern North Dakota is mostly flat prairie land.

Our homestead bordered on the Sioux Indian reservation and was located about 6 or 7 miles from the town of Selfridge. Dad leased some of the Sioux property to enlarge our farm and had a great friendship with the Sioux Chief.

The proximity to town was irrelevant, because the road to our property was more like a trail of ruts made by various vehicles and wagons passing by. It was not reliable in bad weather and certainly not in winter.

The modest creek that ran through our property could become quite a formidable river when snow began to melt, leaving us even more isolated. When it subsided it often left sink holes from which we occasionally had to rescue our errant farm animals.

Our little house was little more than a shack which consisted of three small rooms on the ground floor. The first and most important room was a small kitchen with a wood/coal stove, a table with an odd assortment of chairs and wood boxes for extra seating, a counter for the sink bowl and some shelves with food supplies and unmatched dishes.

Nothing was wasted on the farm. There was a large lidded metal can that we called the slop can that also held an important place in the kitchen. Anything left over such as melon rinds or uneaten food went into that can. When it was fairly full, it was taken out to the pigs. It may have smelled gross to us, but these bacon producers would oink in delight when they saw us coming with that can. I once got knocked over by these enthusiastic slop fans. I was covered with slop and mud. Needless to say, it was a job I tried to avoid at all costs after that distasteful experience.

We had no such thing as running water or electricity. There was a continual need for hot water which was heated in the stove Imagine how hot and muggy the kitchen usually felt? Incredibly, my amazing mom canned and prepared all of our food in that little space. This meant everything from vegetables from the garden to as much as 400 quarts of meat from our farm animals. In addition, dad and mom made their own sausage, churned all of their butter, baked all of their bread and even made their own soap (with ingredients consisting of lye and animal fat. It was a far cry from a Dove bar.)

There was a small porch just outside of the kitchen where we had a milk separator. This separated the milk from the cream so we could later churn butter. We always had loads of cream on everything, which probably accounts for those "healthy" pictures you may have seen of me as a child.

The porch also housed the gas washing machine which was fired up on a weekly basis to wash practically every stitch of clothing and everything else we had, including the well-worn Muslin sheets, embroidered kitchen towels and endless supplies of diapers. If the machine failed, the old method of washing clothes was to boil them on the stove. We hung them out with a hope that we wouldn't have a surprise shower or thunderstorm. Our hopes were often dashed.

The all-important porch served as the only entry to our home, so it was a convenient place for a washbowl filled with water to be used for washing up before we came to the table. No, it wasn't changed between users but remember the lye soap? I am sure even a healthy germ would have trouble surviving that stuff.

We also had a crock filled with water for drinking. There was one dipper that everyone used to drink from We all cleverly tried to drink near the handle, hoping no one else had used that spot.

Besides additional shelves for canned goods, the porch also housed the ever important tub which mom filled with scalding water for those memorable Saturday baths. I volunteered for first bath, always suspecting the inability of my brothers to keep from releasing themselves in the water, To this day, I love a really hot bath.

Mom and Dad and the current baby occupied the only actual bedroom. They had a very small closet because that was all they needed. Under their bed they kept a lidded "pot" which we went in to use when we were sick or when it was too late to go outside to the outhouse. Can you imagine the smell or the job of cleaning it? Mom did that and I never remember it not being clean or ready for use.

At the foot of their bed was a ladder to the attic. The attic was divided into 2 parts. One was the boy's side and the other was the girl's side. The ceiling was so low that an adult could barely stand up straight in the middle. The chimney went up between us and there were some clothes shelves for a barrier. We slept on feather beds which my parents had made, and we were piled high with quilts that mom put together from scraps. Overnight cousins and special friends simply climbed in with us, and when the bed wasn't wide enough, we slept toe to toe with a row at the top and at the bottom. I have slept with more than one pair of stinky feet just a little too close to my nose to enjoy a good night's sleep.

Central heating, for us, meant a coal stove located in the center of the house as our only heat, with exception of the wood/coal kitchen stove which was in continual use. The vents from the house below were opened to let up the heat to the attic at night.

I especially liked these vents because I have never been a good sleeper and I loved to listen to the adult conversations below. Of course, I sometimes filled myself with a lot of mis-information which I had no business sharing, but that did not stop me. No wonder dad called me a chatter box,

No matter what was going on with the weather outside, including those freezing blizzards in North Dakota, the .window beside my bed was always cracked as mom said to let out the "bad "air" Now I know that in that tiny house, we may well have avoided a carbon monoxide build up. Anyway, I still prefer to sleep with an open window.

Of course, we had one other room and that one had more functions than you could imagine. It was a sort of living room with a cot in it. A cot is an especially uncomfortable bed lacking box springs which we used as a couch by day and overnight guests used as a guest bed at night. (This, no doubt, assures that they don't stay too long.)

When anyone was sick, they got to sleep on the cot so we could be nearer mom and dad and, of course, the "pot". This amazing room also served as a dining room when we had guests, and a nursery for orphaned lambs or a chicken hatchery or anything else that needed attention. When my grandma and grandpa came, they got the bedroom and mom and dad slept there on the cot, so it became the master bedroom. Have you ever known of a room with such versatility?

By now you might have guessed that the really important room was no- where near the house. Our little outhouse was located a nice distance away so you got a good morning walk in before breakfast. It also served as a recycling plant, as we used all of our old newspapers and catalogues out there, and today I am sure that everything is composted and nourishing some marvelous plant life. We were green before the term was popular.

Since we had to pump our own water, there was no thought of having any kind of landscaping, except what God had provided. Mom, however, always had a huge and bountiful garden. In the garden was a storm cellar that was used for storing root vegetables, more canned goods, seeds and various garden implements and etc.

Dad hauled ice blocks from the river in the winter, so we were able to make homemade ice cream in the summer. These blocks, covered in straw for insulation, were seasonally stored in the cellar, which kept it all the more cold and damp in the spring. Needless to say this underground abode was also our shelter in event of cyclone, tornado and any kind of a strong wind.

I hated taking refuge in the cellar. With only one door out, I was always sure our house would blow over on the cellar and we would be trapped in there forever. There were no cellphones back then. In fact, like many farmers, we still did not have any phone at all.

We primarily used coal for fuel and fortunately had our own coal bed. Mom and dad would often have to scrape the oil off to get good coal. North Dakota is now a leading producer of oil. We were literally self-sufficient and my dad later said we really did not need money back then.

We had numerous outbuildings such as a chicken coop, a lamb shed, a silo, and of course, the red barn which was also our playground during those long winter months. The barn had a precarious tilt to it. For some reason, it seemed to be directly in a tornado path and had to be pitched back up several times by our good friends and neighbors.

The milk cows, pigs, horses, and assorted other animals found refuge there during those North Dakota winters, The barn and haymow also provided a good place for us kids to get out of moms hair for a while when the weather was just too bad to do anything else. What can be more fun than jumping from the barn into the silo and landing in the soft, soggy, rotting silage?

Overshadowing our barn was a large bluff with rather loose dirt. We transformed it into a wonderful slide by using every imaginable piece of plywood, card board, old blankets or simply our own derrieres. Unfortunately, there were few trousers that could long survive such abuse so it was quite normal for our clothes to be well patched.

We also had our very own wrecking yard and garbage dump. Old farming equipment and broken down cars or trucks were simply put "over the hill" in event they might have useful parts. Besides, there really was no place to get rid of them. Automobiles in those days did not last as long as they do today and were especially vulnerable in hailstorms and blizzards. The few old bottles and cans that were not usable were also buried there.

What fun we had there as kids digging for treasures and dragging broken bottles back to the house or riding the rusted equipment, as we fought imaginary wars, or escaped from bad guys on an old hay bailer or dilapidated truck that had lost its' tires, engine and windows.

During the harsh winters, we sometimes used a horse driven sleigh for transportation. I can still remember going to visit neighbors on a clear cold night snuggled under horsehide blankets and traveling in that old sleigh. Since we had no phones to notify our friends that we were coming, the sleigh bells on a clear night assured that they would have the coffee pot on by the time we got there.

People back then always seemed delighted that the McCay brood had shown up. Farmers shared stories, tips about farming and news while they played games or cards. Kiddies fell asleep on the hostess's bed or floor and sometime late at night we were all carried back to the sleigh and transported home. Socialization was so important on those isolated farms and thinking about it, I believe that friendships ran deeper than they usually do now.

Does it sound like life was difficult for people back in those days? In light of all of our conveniences today, it would be a hard adjustment wouldn't it? But do you know why I feel I was so very blest? I was born into a family where I always knew I was loved and that mom and dad loved each other. I seldom heard an unkind word between them. What a good lesson that is when it comes to making a child feel secure. Remember that how you treat your spouse will have an indelible imprint on your children.

In our home each child was a special blessing. Having a new brother or sister every few years was a whole lot more fun than a bunch of dolls anyway.

I was second oldest with Brother Eddie just 2 years older. By the time I was in 1ˢᵗ grade, Keith, Janice and Loring had also joined our brood. There would be more to come.

For all of the memories and the times I felt welcomed and loved—-I AM GLAD

1 Corinthians 13:8 "Love never fails…"

You will be faced with many struggles and decisions along your own path. No matter what you gain or lose there is nothing that is more important than your love for God (first) and your love for your family (second) and others . No sacrifice is too great to keep what is most important, and that is LOVE.

Family feud

W hile the McCoy's and the Hatfield's were battling it out in the Ozarks, the McCay's and the Dutton's were in a cold war up in North Dakota.

I was so fortunate to have 2 sets of Grandparents who were part of my life. My mom's parents, Pearl and Chester Dutton were amazingly hard working honest farmers who lived around 7 or 8 miles from us. They primarily raised sheep and a little of everything else.

Grandpa Dutton was a difficult and impatient man. Grandma was a short little no nonsense lady with a big smile and a large girth. I will attribute that to her ability to bake long before prepared mixes were available, and her penchant for delectable biscuits and pancakes. She always wore a calico dress and covered it with a large apron (Women did not wear pants back then.) Her sturdy lace up shoes were complemented with long cotton stockings even in the most miserable, humid, and hot North Dakota summers. She wore her graying hair in a long braid which she pinned up on her head and she tied on a sun bonnet whenever she went outside to garden. I thought she was very very old and later realized that she was only in her fifties.

My dad's parents, Georgia and Jesse Hartwell McCay, lived in the capital city of Bismarck in my earliest remembrance. They had also been farmers and were the ones who had actually homesteaded our farm. Grandpa McCay was always into politics and had served in our area as the representative. He later held several government positions. He was forever interested in how to improve the community and the government. He was a stately, wise, and kind gentlemen.

Back in those days, being into politics did not ensure a path to wealth. They lived meagerly in a little duplex with a shared bathroom. Their offspring supplied most of their needs.

Since they lived 70 miles away, it was almost impossible to see them on a regular basis. We seldom had a reliable mode of transportation and besides, we were at war and gas had to be used sparingly.

Though I may be simply delusional, I always felt a special relationship with Grandpa Dutton. I liked going to the Dutton's. It was easy to see where mom had gotten her talent for running a home in far from ideal circumstances. Grandma seemed to know everything about cooking and gardening and her home was immaculate. Grandpa was a virtual workhorse and prided himself on it. I knew this because he seemed to have a disdain for anyone who was not as hardworking and productive as he was.

Whenever I would go to the Dutton's, grandpa would loudly proclaim what a nuisance I was (I told you I was delusional). I remember sitting on his lap and smelling the bleach grandma used so liberally on his overalls mixed with his profuse sweat. I remember too how he declared to grandma that she better hide the cake from me or he'd never see a piece of it himself, and then we would both eat a piece together.

Evenings, Grandpa would tell stories by making shadow figures on the wall with his fingers. I was amazed at how life-like they all looked. This was before the invention of T.V. but he certainly knew how to animate his stories. I never saw a cartoon I enjoyed more.

Mornings, we would come downstairs and find a sculpted animal made out of clay. He insisted that he had no idea where they had come from as he wouldn't waste his time on such nonsense. Of course, I knew it was Grandpa and that behind his tough exterior, he was not only a softy but quite a sculptor.

Grandpa and Grandma Dutton had raised 10 fine healthy and industrious children, but living through those hard times had not been easy. They once lost everything and had to start all over. He had to move the whole family and build a log house to survive in a relatively barren land.

Grandpa expected a lot out of his kids as he needed their help if they were all going to stay alive. Unfortunately, proper parenting skills was not one of his priorities and he often lashed out impatiently saying and doing things I am sure he regretted later. He tried to show his love in other ways.

Mom told me a story later about how she wanted to go to Selfridge and finish High School with other kids her age. The farm was too far away for the daily trip. She said she would work at a hotel for board and room. Grandpa told her that if she left home she couldn't come back.

Well, mom went anyway but in the end Grandpa did welcome her back after High School graduation and that fall he bought her a beautiful coat. That was his way of saying I am sorry. Too bad he couldn't bring himself to say the words too. Despite the fact that he raised honorable and successful children, his words and actions had left a deep hurt, and not all of his children were ever able get over the pain his behavior had caused them.

Young children pick up on a lot of things and being a nosey little character, I heard snatches of conversation early that indicated there was something amiss between the McCay's and the Dutton's. I decided to figure out what it was and fix it. It seemed to have something to do with my dad. I knew the Dutton's hadn't gone to my parents little living room wedding. I also knew that my grandpa admired people who worked hard so I told him that my dad could work harder than he could. He looked at me and said "Ha—your daddy doesn't know noth'n bout work". Then he told my dad what I had said and the next time they worked together, my dad said he nearly killed himself trying to out work Grandpa. My plan had failed.

I finally learned what the problem was between the Dutton's and the McCay's so read on and I'll share it later, but the lessons

I learned from my time with Grandpa was not to judge someone because they are hard on the outside. So often their own hurts have left them unable to allow themselves to be vulnerable. I learned that people who are the most unlovable are often the ones who need love the most, and for that lesson, I AM GLAD

Ephesians 4:2& 3 "Be humble and gentle. Be patient with each other, making allowance for each other's faults because of your love. Always keep yourselves united in the Holy Spirit, and bind yourselves together with peace." (New Living Translation-copyright 1996 by Tyndale press)

You are going to find a few people who are just plain annoying I.e. they have faults. They will need your love even more. You may never know what pain they have gone through in the past, but just as God has given you all His wonderful grace, let us show, that grace to these people.

Santa Fails to Deliver "Fraidy cat"

The first emotion I can distinctly remember is that of fear. There were so many things to be afraid of on that little farm. There were constant warnings to heed and, of course, warnings of the worst possible outcomes were designed as a safety net for a curious pre-school child. Big brother, Eddie liked to call me a "fraidy" cat. (No, you won't find the word in Webster's but you get the idea).

We lived in an area where rattle snakes were so bountiful that Dad and neighbors would actually go into caves in early springs to catch and kill them as they hibernated in huge balls. The rattle snakes proved an eminent threat to livestock and people, so the state gave a bounty for the rattlers in hopes of thinning the unchecked population. Still, every summer we managed to find more than we would have liked.

Any rock or piece of junk should always be examined carefully to be sure a rattle snake was not waiting to pounce on an unlucky child. There were plenty of stories about children and adults who failed to heed such warnings.

A favorite story in our family was about a huge bull snake (the kind that kill rattlers) being found in my parent's bedroom. It disappeared before they could catch it. No one knows how it got in or how it left. I always suspected my attic bedroom window. If a big snake could find its way into our house undetected, why not a rattler?

There was no forgetting the constant howling of coyotes that plagued our area? Any evening trip to the outhouse would be accompanied by their serenade and any time the house quieted at night, they could be heard in the distance awaiting the birth of a helpless calf or yearning for a wandering chicken who had failed to make it to the safety of the chicken coop. Who knew what a hungry pack might do to a child?

What is more frightening than a raging thunderstorm? They are frequent in the Dakotas and everyone seemed to have a story to tell of someone who had been caught finding protection under a tree, or sitting too near a window, or a chimney stove, or mending a fence and then being struck by lightning, No place ever seemed safe from this terrible force.

Thanks to all the information funneled up through that vent in our little house during cold winters, there were also many stories of people who had been caught in a perilous blizzard and froze to death within feet of their home or car. Looking out of our windows at snow piled so high that the landscape was invisible, only confirmed the truth of such fears. Surely we were doomed to a similar fate.

On the endless prairies of the Dakotas and the fact that we were located right next to the vast Sioux reservation meant there were large bands of wild horses that would come thundering through our property at unexpected times. We were duly warned to be on the lookout and take quick cover in a building whenever such an event would happen. Then, I wondered, what if we couldn't make it to a building? Would we be trampled to death?

Tornados and cyclones were to be expected. The storm cellar was our refuge. What if we didn't make it in time? What if the snakes went there for refuge also?

Prairie fires were another source of fear. There was little that could be done when a bolt of lightning or an errant spark kindled a fire. We had no phones and no fire department in the country.

I remember once having to drive through a fire when leaving my grandma Dutton's house. We drove quite quickly as we didn't want the gas from the car to get hot enough to explode. Grandma didn't seemed too concerned about the whole event as she was sure there was enough clearing around the house for the fire to go around. She simply drove off to town for her shopping waiting for the fire to die down before she returned. I was petrified.

My parents were not religious people at the time, but they were good conscientious parents, so my mom would climb up into our attic abode and read Fairy tales to us before we went to sleep at night. Now there is nothing quite as terrifying for a child as the knowledge that there are witches or wolves in the woods that eat little lost kiddies.

Then, of course, I had a big brother who would add to the story through our flimsy barrier. As soon as mom had left, he would assure me that he had seen a witch's house in our woods too. Now of course our woods consisted of little more than a few straggly trees in a gully, but I believed him anyway.

Even more ominous than all of these fears was an even bigger threat.in our life which we had learned from the battery operated radio our parents managed to listen to almost every night. We were in a war! There were bad people who wanted to kill us. They would very likely be sending bombers over our little farm any day. There was no place that we were safe;

One day when I was probably 5 years old my mom came up with a plan that would make us all behave a whole lot better. She told us that there was a Santa Claus and that he could be invisible. He was watching everything we did. In fact, no matter where we went, he would be checking on us. Wow—that was a relief. I would never be alone. I loved the idea.

It wasn't long before I found myself sharing my deepest fears with Santa Claus. If I was sent to gather eggs from the chicken coop, I took Santa along. When I dawdled in the out-house, I shared my fears with Santa. I tattled on my brothers to be sure I gained good favor with Santa. I was sort of a Santa's helper. All that would come to a sad end as you will soon see.

On Christmas Eve, we were all quite excited. Now, we would reap the rewards for not bugging our poor parents or pinching each other when they weren't looking. Santa knew the truth about all of us, and we would be rewarded accordingly.

Brother Eddie was always helping dad and we were pretty sure Santa would be dropping by North Dakota sometime soon, so when they went out to do the evening milking, I decided to tag along to "help" and speed things up. While annoying them with my constant chatter, I noticed a full milk pail and decided to carry it to house for them. I could even add some Santa points with this good deed. Unfortunately, the pail was way too heavy for me to carry any distance so I set it down and ran back to the house to give everyone a progress report.

A little while later Eddie came in with a scowl on his face. Dad was finishing up the chores but he had scolded Eddie for setting the milk pail where the cow would kick it over. I was devastated. All my hard work and good deeds were for naught. I was the one who had put the pail behind the cow. I would need to confess this to dad so that I could redeem myself. I hoped dad would come in before Santa got there.

As the evening dragged on, dad still never came in. We all went upstairs to our attic bedrooms while Mom read Twas the Night Before Christmas. Too late, I heard Santa's reindeer on the roof and I heard Santa yelling, "Whoa Prancer" and "Whoa Dancer" in a voice not too different from dads.

Then Santa managed to come into the house reciting many of our deeds. Wow—He really had been watching us. When

Santa came to me he began to recite what a good helper I was but he never even mentioned that I had just done a very bad deed and hadn't even confessed it yet. While I was relieved, I was even more profoundly disappointed in Santa. Apparently his spirit wasn't really everywhere after all. Had I been talking to myself? Was I really alone after all? It was hard to enjoy my new dolly when it meant that my closest confidante was only a figment of imagination.

Several years later I would learn that there really is a Spirit and Confidante that can be with us at all times. We can talk to Him. We can pray to Him. He cares so much about us. I will always remember what it is to feel alone and to have no knowledge of a Heavenly Father for it makes the real story all the more awesome.. We are created to have fellowship with God. The difference between not knowing this and knowing this makes the reality such a wonderful revelation and so for the times of loneliness and the contrast they provided, I AM Glad.!

Matthew 28:20b Lo, I am with you always, even to the end of the age. Hebrews 13:5 I will never leave you or forsake you.

Miss Bossy goes to Bismarck

B irth order made a major contribution to how our family
worked By the time I had reached the ripe old age of 6,
there were 5 children in our family. Eddie age 8 and myself,
were always referred to as the big kids. Keith and Janice were
middle kids

And Loring and Rodney (who joined us later) were always
the little kids. The middle kids seemed to be moved up to big
kids or down to little kids depending on the circumstances.

Being one of the big kids meant Eddie and I had both more
responsibilities and more privileges. Eddie was dad's right hand
on the farm. He had Grandpa Dutton's penchant for hard work
and dad often said how invaluable he was. Then there was me.

While, I liked to think I was mom's big helper, I was probably more of a nuisance with my constant chatter. Girl's work
was gathering eggs from the henhouse or wherever else our
free roaming chickens had decided to lay them, scrubbing
dirty socks on the scrub board until they qualified for the wash

machine, helping with the littler kids, assisting with getting the wash on and off the lines (we were solar) and anything around the kitchen.

One of my jobs was setting the table. We had no such thing as matching dishes or silverware, so I carefully chose the place settings to match the people. The big green cracked plate was always reserved for the biggest eater and the dainty little rose plate was saved for special guests like my pretty Aunt Mildred.

I think I helped mom most by watching the "little /middle" ones while she ran out to do something with dad or simply needed some of us out from under her feet while she canned or had some other task that she needed a break from. She expressed her appreciation and I loved the job because I truly adored my siblings and enjoyed taking care of them. They, in turn, probably thought I had exceeded my authority on more than one occasion.

One day the summer before I had quite turned 6, Grandma Dutton arrived with a bag of used clothing which included some of grandpa's red long johns. These, she said, would give mom something to work with to get Gladys ready for school.

My goodness! I was going to school. I knew that school meant I would have to go to Bismarck because there was no school near us and Eddie and 2 of our teenage cousins already stayed with Grandma and Grandpa McCay winters to attend school. At 70 miles distance and incompatible roads, Bismarck was a world away.

First mom carefully cut out the least worn parts of the used clothing to make me a couple of school dresses and then she cut grandpa's long johns up for some proper warm underwear for me. All this would be accomplished on our faithful sewing machine which was self- powered by a foot treadle. What a great exercise that was! No wonder mom was always trim and fit.

Meanwhile, I fretted. How in the world was Mom going to get by without me? Who would take the little /middle ones to the outhouse and help train them? Who would fetch the diapers?

What would the little/middles do without their big bossy sister? We would soon find out.

All of my fears seemed to come to a head when we all packed up and left for Bismarck. Weren't we in a war? Would Bismarck be bombed? Would my cousins like me? How would I fit in in a big school with a bunch of strangers?

While grandma and grandpa lived in a three room duplex, there was a basement for food storage, the wash machine, indoor clothesline, a furnace, and, of course, stray grandchildren. Dad and grandpa simple put a heavy green curtain between the teen girl cousins and our abode.

Eddie and I each had a cot near the furnace so we were usually warm enough. Being teenagers, my cousins took advantage of the clothesline and the furnace to dry their more delicate laundry so we had some interesting décor to negotiate.

Cousin Audrey was quite patient with her young cousins but Cousin Loretta found us to be a real pain. It was an awkward situation and a learning experience. We were camping in enemy territory as far as we were concerned.

Somehow, the noisy clatter of the furnace during those winter nights felt comforting and it drowned out the sound of the occasional planes overhead. My imagination assured me that they were all enemy planes, so the less I heard them, the better.

To make matters worse, we actually had blackout curtains in event of an air raid. I am not sure if we ever used them, but the idea that it might be necessary was plenty scary. A trip to the movies always showed pictures from the war. Some were of England and the streets that were being pummeled by enemy aircraft. Would we be next??

Having a real indoor bathroom, though communal with the neighboring duplex, was an exhilarating experience at first. However since we shared our bathroom with no less than 10 people, it had to be left clean and no one was allowed to lag. Baths were scheduled and toilet paper carefully monitored. Unfortunately, there was more than one problem for grandma to resolve between the neighbors and her grandkids concerning proper bathroom etiquette.

For the first time in my life, we actually had electricity. It was used sparingly. No one accidentally left a room and neglected to pull the chain that would turn the lonely little light bulb or small lamp off, Both grandma and grandpa were well up into their seventies with this odd assembly of grandkids to watch after. They were always long-suffering and uncomplaining despite this huge responsibility.

Grandpa spent his days down at the capitol building just seeing what those "fools" were up to now. His days in government were over, but his interest never waned. Interestingly North Dakota had a population of just under 700.000 when grandpa was a representative. That is still the approximate census. Grandpa was a gentleman and dressed like one every single day. He smoked a pipe and used a cane. He always smiled and spoke kindly to us as though what we had to say was truly interesting. Grandpa's driving was another issue. He was self-taught and he made up his own rules as he went. He was a diligent honker. Everyone else who managed to barely miss us was another "fool". Apparently not every fool was down at the capitol.

When Grandpa was home he occupied the one comfortable chair in the small living room. He read the paper and he listened to war reports on his static prone radio. He always knew what "our boys" were doing and what the next war effort would be.

Grandma never said an unkind word that I can remember. She had lived a very tough life and she was thankful for anything she ever had. Just a few years before she had lived with grandpa and 3 of their children on the McCay homestead property in a 10 by 12 house. This little duplex must have felt quite grand to her and she also proved to be one of those remarkable people that we all love to be around: a person who truly appreciates everything about life.

Grandma dressed properly too. She had several dresses of a soft jersey material, which she wore daily, covered by a huge apron. Grandma seldom left the house. She gardened, cooked and did the wash. Ice was delivered for our Ice box as needed. Much of the pantry was stocked by her children, who visited as weather and roads permitted. She had born 8 children (four of them farmers) who clearly loved their parents. She simply "made do" with whatever she got.

School was everything I had dreaded. The city kids were different. My life was different. My homemade clothes were different. My over protective grandma made me bundle in both long underwear and long brown stockings which I was sure made me look like a stuffed sausage.

I had memorized the first readers that Eddie had brought home for the summer and read to me, so the teacher thought I could already read and when she discovered I couldn't, I was embarrassed and she was chagrined. I had a lot of make up to do to catch up.

When I finally did learn to read, I loved it. We had to buy our books back then. There was a Dick and Jane series that was prominent in all the schools. It was generally a propaganda book for parents on how children should always help and do the right thing. I noticed that when Jane set the table, she used matching dishes. When Father came home from work, he had a tie on. Mother was always dressed in high heels. Baby Sally had a little peddle car that she rode around the neighborhood on nice cement sidewalks.

We, McCay's, were definitely behind the times. I began to dream of a Dick and Jane life. I didn't see Jane chasing chickens off the porch, playing on old hay balers, or scrubbing socks on a scrub board.

I had not been there very long when grandma let me in on a secret. She was going to let Eddie and me go to Sunday school. I had never been to Sunday school. Our family was not the religious sort. Now I suspect grandma, sweet as she was, might have wanted a little peace from us, but nevertheless, I was so excited. Eddie told me I better keep my big trap shut about the whole thing. On that very first day, grandpa dropped us off and were allowed to walk home.

Sunday school was an amazing experience. The teacher was so nice. She told us that somebody named Jesus loved us. I wondered if that was a relative I hadn't met yet. She said he died for us. I thought maybe he was in the war like my cousin Don. We sang songs and we prayed for our country. We took up an offering to help do God's work. I put in the 3 pennies grandma had given me. Another girl put in a 50 cent piece. Wow, I wished I could do that. Even with World War 11 prices, I wasn't sure I could help God much with only 3 pennies.

It took a while for me to get the concept of a God we could actually pray to. I hoped he was a better bet than Santa Claus had been. Could God really put an end to the War? Did he really care about a little girl who was scared of everything and often laid awake until the roosters began to crow, just to be sure she had been kept through another night?

No matter what, I could hardly wait for each Sunday to come around. The big flannel board came alive with astonishing stories every Sunday. Moses crossing the Red Sea and David killing the giant were favorites.

Well, if you don't know what a flannel board is, I should tell you. Long before DVD's and Videos and T.V., people would draw scenic backgrounds on a flannel material and then tell a story by placing paper cutouts on the flannel board until the picture was complete. This kept us in rapt attention and I have more vivid memories of these than any cartoon I later saw.

A whole school year away from home seemed like such a long time. There was gas rationing because of the war and mom and dad mostly drove an old pickup, so a visit was rare. Roads, of course, were not always passable during the winter anyway.

Finally, in what seemed like forever, our family came to see Eddie and me. I remember how awkward I felt. My younger siblings had grown quite nicely without my help. They had changed and so had I. Well, I felt different anyway. I had been exposed to the sophisticated world of Dick and Jane. I knew how life was supposed to be.

When mom and dad left, they gave us each a whole dollar. That was a lot of money in those days. A bottle of pop was 10 cents and a movie was 15 cents. A large candy bar was only 5 cents.

I decided to take my whole dollar and give it as an offering at Sunday school. Now lest you think I was such a Godly little Christian, I must admit that my motive was more to trump the little girl who always brought a 50 cent piece. Apparently the teacher had not given the lesson Jesus taught about giving in secret, rather than like the Publicans did to impress.

I took my dollar and flashed it around, even dropping it to be sure everyone noticed it. Finally the offering came and I gave it one last wave in the air and placed it in the offering. God would certainly have a lot to work with this week!

I was walking home from Sunday school when reality hit. I would have no more spending money until mom and dad came to pick us up at the end of the school year. There would be no special treats. I would have to depend on grandma for pennies again. I had a case of givers remorse. I sure hoped God was enjoying my money.

By the end of the school year, I had actually made a few friends. I wasn't allowed to go to any ones house as grandma worried so much. However, some of the girls in the neighborhood would come over and we would play jump rope or hopscotch. We always talked about the war because everyone had somebody who was fighting in the war somewhere. Our own dad did not get drafted because he was a wheat farmer and it was a needed crop. That was one good reason to be a farmer!

Amazingly, just as my life changed again, so did the war. Germany surrendered the first of May just before the end of the school year. There was joy beyond belief. We were all

Americans and we were united in our ecstasy. Of course Japan was still holding out in the Pacific, but now we had hope. We were sure the war would end there too. Had God answered our Sunday school prayers? I wondered.

Finally, one day in Mid-May, our mom and dad arrived to take us home. By this time I had serious doubts about the viability of farm life. It hadn't seemed to bring us all that much in comparison to the city dwellers. I had been exposed to the good life; an indoor bathroom and electric lights. My life would never be the same again.

The whole year had been an adventure. I was often scared and lonely. Now I knew what it was like not to be readily accepted, I had been the obnoxious little cousin at home and the backward farm girl dressed in a strange assortment of home-made clothing at school.

There was one place I had felt accepted though, and for my first remembrance of Sunday School and the love I felt from a Sunday School teacher, whose name I cannot even recall, and the message that began to permeate my heart, I AM GLAD;

Galatians 6:9-10 "And let us not grow weary of doing good, for in due season we will reap, if we do not lose heart. Therefore as we have opportunity, let us do good to everyone, and

especially to those who are of the household
of faith".

I am sure my Sunday school teacher never knew what
happened to that little farm girl with the faded homemade
clothes, well -worn brown shoes and frayed pigtails; the one
who fidgeted in class and sometimes talked out of turn. Neither
will you know what happens to everyone you encourage, teach,
give to, or mentor. Keep on. Don't give up. Just remember, you
may never see the reward for what you do here on earth, but
neither would you want to miss helping someone whose life
could be changed.

Home Again

Back home again, the one thing I knew I would really miss was Sunday school, and despite Eddie's dire warning for me to keep my trap shut, those chances were slim to none. We were barely home when I informed my family that we should say a prayer before we ate. My normally gentle dad expressed his displeasure and wanted to know where I had gotten such an idea. Of course the secret was out and I felt like I had betrayed grandma. It was obvious my suggestion was not well received. In fact, I often blamed myself for the next decision my dad made. We would not be going away to school again. He and the neighbors were putting up a little one room school house for us to attend at a central location between several farms. So much for city life!!

Sometime that summer I learned that our teacher would be our very own Cousin Audrey. Yes, the same one who lived with us at grandmas. She was just a teenager but she had passed a state test for an emergency credential. While I felt sorry for us,

I felt even sorrier for her. What teenager wants to be stuck out in the middle of nowhere teaching her errant cousins?

Summer dragged on and so did the Asian Pacific War. With our battery operated radio our parents were able to keep up with the news. The Japanese had not surrendered as soon as we had expected.

With the same radio, they also listened to Jack Benny and another program called Fiber Mcgee and Molly, which was great clean comedy. It's amazing how the old radio programs could actually be so funny because we had to listen intently and then put the pictures in our imagination. It was at least a temporary reprieve from the ominous stories of the war we were engaged in.

Saturdays we had our weekly baths and went to town. Dad actually rigged a shower up in the coal shed (pretty empty for summer) by putting an old barrel on the roof and letting the water out with some sort of a sprinkler. The barrel in the sun warmed the water so we had our solar water heater. Too bad he didn't patent it.

Town consisted of Smesteds' General store, the granary, a few hotels with bars, a couple of churches several filling stations with garages, because cars were always in need of repairs back then, and little else. An occasional movie would be shown at the grange hall on fold out seats;

We bought everything at Smesteds from shoes to incidentals. They actually had 3 flavors of ice cream that summer. What a treat it was to have a choice between chocolate, strawberry and vanilla. There was nothing more delectable than a double deck cone on a warm Saturday night in Selfridge.

Everyone knew mom and dad in Selfridge and that made us feel special. It was a time to gather a few supplies, catch up on local events, and get some needed socialization. Unfortunately, it was also a time for some young men to get their pay checks for working on some of the farms or money for their farm goods and head for the bar. How sad to work so hard and drink up all the profits.

In mid-summer some real excitement hit. We were in for a tornado. My Aunt Helen arrived in her old car with her 2 babies from a neighboring farm. She had no storm cellar and our cellar was the safest place she could think of. We all squeezed into our scary, stuffy, garden cellar, hoping not to meet any rattlesnakes down there. Luckily we did have a flashlight.

Soon we heard the winds howl and the crashing and pounding of what seemed like tons of debris flying over our cellar. Would we be able to get out? Would anything be standing? What would we do if our farm was gone? Worse yet, what if we didn't survive either? In the midst of the chaos I remembered how the Sunday school teacher had taught us to pray. I decided to close my eyes and try it. Soon the winds calmed down and I thought it was kind of the like a story she had told of how Jesus had calmed the sea. Maybe it was He who had helped us.

With the calm, we all gingerly raised the cellar door and peeked out. Our house was still standing and intact. As usual, the barn had blown down, but we knew friends and relatives would come and help us put it back up again. That's just the way it was back then.

The next morning we climbed into our old pickup and went around to see where we could help. We found a little family who had taken refuge at Grandpa and Grandma Dutton's farmhouse. We went to see if their house was still standing. Only box springs and a pair eyeglasses were left. It was impossible to tell that a house had ever been there. Thankfully, no one we knew was hurt but there was going to be some real work to do to restore our little farm community.

In the middle of all this, we had the most incredible news. We had dropped 2 atomic bombs on Japan. The war was over. We didn't even know the government had such a powerful bomb. We felt sorry for the people who were hurt, but we were glad our boys would be coming home. The war was over, but I had another fear and that was the atomic bomb. I sure hoped that the government was guarding our supply.

Summer is a time for immense work on the farm. All the crops had to be tended to. The cattle had to be branded and the sheep sheared. Wheat and corn were harvested. A hail storm or a windstorm could change everything. We lived on the edge and every jar mom canned and every animal dad butchered were one more assurance that we could make it through another year.

Eddie worked like a little man, but I fear I took advantage of the fact that I was a girl. Somehow in the midst of every-thing, mom and dad both honored the position of a lady, which was apparently their dream for what I would become. Certain things like milking our 21 milk cows was off limits. Of course, I wanted to be where the action was so I sat on the fence and watched while Eddie and then Keith milked the cows by hand. They managed to spray me more than once.

Extra cream made in our back porch separator and eggs from mom's chickens were taken to town for sale, as were other crops like wheat and barley. Of course, the town had a granary where we would take our grain in the fall and come back with sacks of flour from what we didn't sell.

I always loved to ride in the bed of the combine and feel the wheat fall over me during the fall harvest. Now I wonder, "what lucky housewife served up cakes made from flour that had come from our wheat, after hosting a dirty little farm girl"?

When we had time, we barrel walked, which was something the occasional farm hands had taught us. We simply climbed up on barrels and tried to walk without falling off. We also took old fence posts or boards and nailed cans to them and made stilts. Slivers and bumps were common. Mom often got out the iodine and poured it on where ever we had been stuck or wounded. The cure was more painful than the injury.

We always needed extra help during harvest, and there were young men available for just that. These youthful men always fascinated us and they had plenty of stories to tell. They also liked to wrestle each other and a few liked to show their questionable manhood by handling our plentiful supply of snakes.

An impromptu rodeo would occasionally ensue when a fresh colt or one of the horses selected from the wild horses that ran through our property needed to be broken. My dad was a skilled cowboy and I was so proud to sit up on the fence and watch him break a horse.

Of course, we had our own horses to ride, but that was no big deal to us. My own horse, old Nellie, was blind in one eye and wouldn't go very far from the farm without stubbornly turning around and going back. She was like me. She didn't want to be too far from the feeding trough.

Summer ended and we began the adventure of walking to our own school. This time Keith joined the big kids even though he was really too young to go to first grade. I imagine this helped boost the numbers for the school as we only had 14 students in grades 1 through 8.

School was one room with a stove in the middle for heat. There was also a lean to building for coal and a few emergency supplies in case we ever got stuck there in a blizzard. We had no shade trees and no playground equipment. Of course, we did have that all important outhouse which happened to get tipped over on Halloween night. Grandma Dutton said some scalawags did it.

Since there was no cement area, many games like hopscotch or jacks just couldn't be played. One recess we all decided to race down the hill and around an old dead cow that we had noticed for several days. To our surprise, the cow was not dead at all. She was laying on her side moaning and trying to give birth. Eddie and his farm buddies simply took over and delivered the little calf. They knew just what to do and soon there was a baby calf and a very happy cow. Now who gets that kind of adventure in recess today?

Every morning we would pack our lunches and wrap them in wax paper. My favorite sandwich was homemade bread with homemade butter and real sugar. Mom had also found something called Kraft Salad Dressing that she bought and sometimes that was our sandwich filling. It was also used for the dressing on lettuce. Now living on a farm we had plenty of fresh vegetables in the summer and canned vegetables in the winter so we were far from deprived,

Breakfast was often homemade biscuits or pancakes piled with sausage gravy. Farmers can really eat heartily because they work so hard. Dinner was actually our noon meal and supper, a lighter fare was for dinner.

My very favorite dinner meal was fresh home fried chicken, potatoes and gravy. Colonel Sanders couldn't compete with mom on this one.

Back then, when you cooked a chicken, you cooked the whole thing. There was no choosing a package of chicken breasts or thighs. Chickens aren't made that way. As a result, everyone had their favorite piece and we all hoped it wasn't picked before you got the platter.

Strangely, my mom always chose the chicken back claiming it was her very favorite piece. She even ate the liver and the gizzard. Years later I realized what an act of love that really was. She wanted the rest of us to have the best.

We never actually had to spend the night in the schoolhouse but one day a blizzard did move in. Dad fired up an old tractor and rescued us. He couldn't take the short route we walked because it was impassable by vehicle. He simply took a long route along the crop land and arrived just as the snow was coming down pretty heavy.

We all held on to dad as he took off, trusting that he could somehow drive through the blinding snow to our little home on the prairie. I knew dad loved us very much to take such a risk to get us home, but my old fears gripped me again when I peeked over his shoulder and could not even see a familiar landmark. I wondered if God really did know where we were. Just in case, I closed my eyes and said a little prayer again.

Well, home looked pretty good after that adventure. It occurred to me that Dick and Jane probably never had to ride home on a tractor during a blizzard.

What an eventful year we were having. The war was finally over! People had gas to travel more and when I think about it now I believe that, for me, the most important thing that had happened was that little bit of faith that had been planted in me by my Sunday School teacher. Whenever anything happened, I wondered if God was in it. Somehow, life wasn't quite as scary as it had been.

For the realization that perhaps prayer could make a difference I AM GLAD

Mark 11:24&25 Whatever things you ask when you pray believe that you will receive.......If you have anything against anyone, forgive him, that your Father in heaven may also forgive your trespasses.

What a wonderful privilege we have to pray to the Creator of the universe and know that he hears us. Just a little reminder though. God forgave us of our sins against him—we must also remember to forgive anyone who has offended us in any way. You will have plenty of opportunity to practice this verse. I have found, that if we not only forgive others, but also pray for them, it is just amazing how soon we forget the offense, and begin to genuinely love them.

Big Changes Down on the Farm

As soon as the war ended, things began to change quite rapidly. Towards the end of second grade, dad had gone out and bought a big generator and powered our house with real electric lights. Of course, the many wires to accomplish this meant strings of electrical cords everywhere and a generator setting on the porch just below my window that would go off and on as needed often nearly shaking the house down at 3:00 in the morning. The McCay's were moving up!

Later that spring, another astounding thing happened. We actually got a genuine new two tone, brown and tan, Chevy sedan. No more piling in the back of the pickup to ride to town or family gatherings. We were so excited. Never mind that car air conditioner had not yet been invented and heaters were optional.

Of course, we did not have the luxury of a car radio either, but with 5 lively children, who could have heard it anyway?

Back then there were also no signals on cars. Drivers simply rolled down their windows, (there were handles for that) even in the worst of weather, and we all joined dad by making copycat signals by hand to indicate stopping or turning, We must have looked like a big caterpillar and I am sure mom did not appreciate the extra dousing we all got during a good rain, but she understood our new car delirium.

One day in early spring we went to town to pick up our mail (of course we didn't have mail delivery where we lived—those mailman might go through rain, sleet, and snow to deliver mail, but those old roads of ours were just too much) and mom had a letter from her brother who lived in Washington. It seems that they were coming back to North Dakota and would like to stay with us some of the time while they visited family and preached a revival, whatever that was. Gas rationing was over and people were traveling again.

Mom was so excited. She loved her brother, Gerald. Dad was a little more dubious. What in the world would a preacher want to stay at our house for? Of course mom pointed out how he was a favorite brother and this would be a perfect place because he had two kids and they could play with us. My ears perked up on that.

Wow- We had cousins I had never met. That was an exciting turn of events. I could hardly wait.

Uncle Gerald and Aunt Selma arrived with pretty little brown eyed Sharon, who was 2 years younger than I, and brother "Merky" who was just a year younger but, at least it seemed, a lot wiser in the ways of the world than we farm kids. After all, we had never been anywhere but the Dakotas and he was all the way from the Pacific Ocean.

In no time at all, I was filling little Sharon with tall tales of life on the prairie. I was certainly glad there was no Santa to be listening in on these or I would have had a whole lot of confessing to do. I just knew life was far too boring on our Dakota farm to interest anyone who had actually been anywhere else so I decided it was my responsibility to spice it up a bit. (Shame on me). I just reasoned that they already had a far more exciting life than I did. Besides, I was quite envious of them. They all got to get dressed up and go to the "revival" while we stayed home and milked cows and fetched eggs.

One day Sharon decided it was her duty to let me know why Grandpa and Grandma Dutton didn't have much use for my dad. I was all ears. This had been a mystery all my life.

Sharon matter-of-factly informed me that we, McCays, were bad people, so we were going to a very bad place where it was very dark and hot and we would stay for ever and ever. Oh My—that sounded like we were going to be stuck in that dreadful storm cellar I always hated. Anyway, I wondered what was so bad about us because a lot of people in town seemed to like us. She said that the Dutton's believed in God and we didn't, so we were in a lot of trouble. She thought for a while and then added the clincher, just in case not believing in God wasn't enough. She said that we played cards and we went to movies and we drank beer and stuff. At least that is all the information she had heard.

Hmm, I certainly didn't want to have to spend forever and forever in a place like that cellar alone. It was so much fun to have company so I decided to take her with me. I knew where dad kept the whiskey in the cellar so I took her down and gave her a swig. There, just in case she was right, I would always have someone to listen to my endless Dakota jargon.

For a few days I pondered why the McCay's didn't believe in God but the Dutton's did. I guess my mom was beginning to think the same thing. She began to pester my dad to go and hear Gerald preach, while dad complained that summer was no time to hold a revival. "Didn't Gerald have the sense to know that farmers had no time to spare in the summer—why didn't Gerald come in the winter to hold his revival?"

Well, just in case they hadn't thought of it, I decided to volunteer the information that no one could get to town in the winter for a revival anyway. One look from dad and I knew that was exactly what he was thinking too. So much for my ideas.

Now mom was smart. She didn't cry over any old thing but saved her tears for special occasions. The occasion had arisen. After all, her brother had come all the way from Washington to preach. Besides mom used to go to church herself and she kinda missed it. How could dad make a decision if he never even listened to him?

When dad couldn't take another tear, he decided that he would go, just once, but the kids didn't need to go and hear all that bunk. It would just confuse them. Being smarter, he could handle it, so off they went while we stayed home to tend the farm for the evening.

We were all fast asleep before dad and mom got home and we had no idea what was in store the next morning. Our lives would be forever changed.

We came down for a big breakfast like mom always made, but before we could start our customary gobbling, dad said we should pray first. Was he kidding? Since when did we pray? Maybe he was making fun of Uncle Gerald. Dad always liked to joke. I bowed my head like I learned to do in Sunday school, but I peeked at dad just in case. Then the miraculous happened. Dad actually prayed. It wasn't a big fancy prayer liked the preacher at my uncle Lester's funeral, but it was a prayer just the same.

Needless to say that was a whole new chapter in our life. We begin to arise early enough to have "family worship". This meant reading out of a Bible Story book because dad simply knew very little about what the Bible said so we were all beginning together. We were spellbound with all the stories and oh how we loved to pray. It was so much fun to be a Christian family!

We learned how God had created a wonderful world and then put us in it to love and enjoy but a terrible thing happened. God had also created a beautiful angel named Lucifer. He rebelled against God and someday he will be destroyed forever, but right now He is trying to get all of us to join in the rebellion .He causes trouble everywhere. People began to follow Lucifer because He promised more fun but He was really tricking people into destroying their own lives and relationship with God. You see, God has rules to protect us and to make the world a wonderful place. When we don't follow his rules, everything gets worse and worse

Even though people rebel against God, He still wants to save us, He knew that death would be the right punishment for people who chose to disobey and that was everybody! He still loved us and decided to send His own Son to die instead of us. If we can believe His Son Jesus and what He did for us and chose to follow Him we can someday live with Him forever. Dad and mom had made that choice.

Dad was so enthralled with his new life as a believer that he never wanted to miss a single revival service. Once when, for some reason we had no other way to get to church, he actually hooked up a 2 wheel wagon to the tractor, packed us all in with blankets and headed the 7 miles to town for church. What a slow ride that was but we loved it too.

Now we could get dressed up and go to church like other people. For the first time in our life we were exposed to congregational singing and the old hymns. I remember figuring out that the song, There is Power in the Blood meant that Jesus had died for us and that when we believed in him, that blood had power. It had certainly changed things around our home.

Now that we were going to church, I got my very first store bought dress. Oh, I was so proud. It was blue taffeta which promptly faded in the sun to a sort of lavender. To assure that everyone knew it was store bought, I refused to let the tags be removed. My brothers had great fun with my tags and I was often tattling how they were pulling on them.

For the first time in our life, we got to go to a real Vacation Bible School. There we learned more about Jesus and we also learned more about His enemy, Lucifer who we call the devil and how he wanted to destroy us. Well, that certainly wasn't good news! However it didn't take long for us to see just how the old devil works.

Just about the time Vacation Bible ended my dad was trying to break one of the horses that he had singled out from the wild horses that came through our property. The horse that we had named Black Beauty knocked my dad up against a fence and before we knew it, dad had a huge gash on his leg that would lay him up for at least a week during very crucial farm time. Luckily, brother Eddie was a really big help and the relatives and neighbors came over to pitch in.

No sooner was dad back to work when he took sick. Mom soon realized that this sickness was a whole lot worse than a summer flu bug and she packed him up to drive him to a hospital in Bismarck, 70 miles away.

We stayed home with a lady mom got from town to watch us. It didn't take long for us to wear her down and she quit and headed back to civilization!

This was in the dreadful years before Jonas Salk had invented the polio vaccine. There was a polio epidemic across the country. Many people died and many others wound up paralyzed and in wheel chairs for the rest of their lives. Special sanatoriums were set up just for people with polio and Bismarck had one. You guessed it! Dad had polio. What a bummer!

Soon after dad was admitted to the sanatorium, mom came home to check on us. She was barely there when someone drove out from town with a message. There had been a phone call to the post office to deliver a message about my dad. The message was that he had passed away. (Truly the message was originally to get back to Bismarck to be with dad when he passed away but someone took the liberty to update the message assuming he had surely died by then.) Mom turned white and jumped back in the car to go back to Bismarck.

Ironically, a very strange thing happened. My normal fear left. We had just learned about how Jesus had raised Lazarus from the dead in our Bible Story. Now we were Christians. Wouldn't He do the same for us if we asked him? We went right in and prayed that God would raise dad up. Do you know what? A miracle did happen and I will never forget it. When mom got to the sanatorium, dad was not only alive and alert but he was looking for his clothes, so he could get back to the farm.

Of course dad had a ways to gain his strength back and he had lost a lot of weight, but by summer's end he was perfectly healthy. I had learned something that would make a difference for the rest of my life. God really does care for us. He really does want the best for us. God answers prayers and he still does miracles and I AM GLAD.

Psalms 18:30 & 31 "As for God, His way is perfect: the word of the Lord is proven; He is a shield to all who trust in Him."

Ephesians 3:17-19 "…that Christ may dwell in your hearts through faith that you, being rooted and grounded in love, may be able to comprehend with all the saints what is the width and length and depth and height to know the love of Christ which passes knowledge, that you may be filled with all the fullness of God."

There will be times of darkness and discouragement in all of your lives. Never forget the wonderful times and the miracles God has done in your past and you will be reminded that He can and will do the same again.

The Moving McCay's

Things were moving quickly at the McCay's. By fall dad had decided that we needed to sell the very farm his family had homesteaded. He wanted to be in a place that we could all go to church regularly. Our little church in Selfridge was often without a pastor and the fact that we lived several miles out of town, with impassable roads during bad weather, meant that we couldn't always be there anyway.

Before Uncle Gerald had gone back to Washington, he had assured mom and dad that it would be a beautiful place to resettle. Both mom and dad were up for the adventure.

As soon as the crops were in, we had a big auction and sold everything but enough to pack in a little green trailer, and we headed for Washington. My brothers cried, but I was beside myself with joy. Now, I was sure we would be moving to a city like Dick and Jane from my 1st grade primer. My dad would probably get a job where he would wear a suit every day, and mom would always be dressed up like we usually just dressed for church. I would set the table in matching dishes while my brothers would help father (the much more sophisticated title than dad or daddy) mow the lawn and rake the leaves instead of slopping pigs and milking those smelly cows. Most importantly, we would have a real indoor bathroom. Yes, we were moving up!

We arrived in beautiful Washington in October and lived in a big old farmhouse which we shared with Uncle Gerald and his family, for most of that winter. Sure enough, we did have an indoor bathroom which was huge because it had once been a bedroom and was converted with the recent addition of indoor plumbing.

What an adventure we were having! Dad and mom took us to see the ocean and we were driving distance to snow covered Mount Baker. Mom said that was the way she liked her snow—at a distance! We did have snow but nothing like North Dakota.

We enrolled in Ferndale Elementary School and rode the bus to school in town. I supposed we would be moving to town any day, as soon as my dad got his job so I was busy trying to figure out how to best fit in. I imagined that I would need a whole new wardrobe as soon as possible. My one store bought dress had seen its best days by now, and my homemade North Dakota attire was pretty shabby next to my new classmates.

Soon dad and mom were out looking for a farm to buy. Well, that certainly wasn't in my plans, but the pretty little dairy's I saw from the school bus did look inviting. Maybe a two story white house with green shutters, like a fourth grader on our bus lived in would work. I sure hoped that one would come up for sale.

Thank goodness, no one seemed to have outhouses except for one poor family who lived on the bus route. I felt so sorry for them. Their house was just pathetic. It was just a tiny low ceiling shack with brown shingle siding on the front and unpainted boards the rest of the way around. The ram shackle outhouse was located far away from the house next to some other old out-buildings. In fact, the barn was the only good thing about their little farm and even it needed a paint job.

One day mom and dad said they had a surprise for us. They had found a farm and they wanted to show us our new home. Of course, there was still plenty to do like buy cows and all to make it a real dairy, but we would be moving soon. Mom was pregnant again and we needed to get settled.

Off we went after school one day to visit our newly acquired dairy. Would you believe it? It was that same dinky little pathetic house on our bus route. This was terrible news! I remember walking into the little two bedroom, would-be cottage, and noting how low the stained ceiling was, how uneven the floor was and how it smelled like mildew and mice.

Yuck! I was panicky. North Dakota was beginning to seem like a better place. At least everyone knew us back there. Who would ever want to come and visit us here?

Well, in no time at all mom was busy cleaning and painting. While dad and Eddie took care of the farm stuff like cows and all, she managed to get some ply board and put up a partition and a small closet to make a girl's bedroom and a boy's bedroom out of one small bedroom.

Thanks to bunk beds, mom and dad were cleverly able to accommodate 5 kids in a space of about 12 by 12 at the most. The girl's side was papered with pink floral and the boys with blue airplanes. What more could we ask for?

Our only heat was a pot belly wood stove in the living room. A good paint job and plugging up some old holes cut down on mice traffic and the addition of mom's good cooking made the place smell a lot better. Window boxes on the outside front were planted in pansies. A dilapidated porch would accommodate mom's canned goods and our good old stainless steel tub for those Saturday night baths!

We did have real electricity, a phone, and running water in the kitchen and, more importantly, the rather modern barn. While mom and dad basked in their good fortune, I fretted about the old outhouse in plain view of the school bus. I was definitely more concerned about image than the viability of the dairy.

Sure enough, we were able to move before school was out and it was now the pathetic McCay's that had to board the school bus in the inquisitive and sometimes judgmental view of our bus mates. Predictably, there were a few mean girls on the bus who held their nose when we got on. (I guess they would be called bullies today). They laughed at our outhouse and made some snide remarks about my clothes. They called my house the shoe house because of the little nursery rhyme about the old women in the shoe who had so many children she didn't know what to do. (The house was so small, that with all of us piling out for the school bus, it must have seemed that way.)

No, I did not have to go into therapy to overcome those grievous times. In fact, some of my best memories were planted in that little house in the Washington woods. In a twist of irony, one of the "mean" girls developed a big crush on brother Eddie. That certainly shsssed them up.

In that little house, I learned that a real home is not built on what it looks like from the outside, but on the love that is inside of it, and I AM GLAD.

1 Corinthians 13:13 And now abide faith, hope, love, these three; but the greatest of these is love.

You will not be starting your life or your family in the kind of beautiful homes that you all grew up in. You may never achieve your dream house or your dream job, but the best memories you can have, and that you can give, will always be those times when love abounded and selfish ambitions were absent.

A Spanking to Remember

T hird grade was out for the summer, and what a year it had been! Fall had started in a one room schoolhouse located near our modest farm in North Dakota and by the end of the year we had relocated to our little dairy in Washington. Neither place would be featured on the home tour, unless the editor was on the lookout for the few places that still had outdoor bathroom accommodations A.K.A. outhouses.

Unfortunately, our fortune had not come to fruition either. When it was learned that a few farms over actually hired children to work in the strawberry fields that were so often merged between the little dairies, it was decided that this would be a grand experience for us.

As soon as Eddie, age 10, was done helping dad get all the cows milked he was sent off with Keith, age 7 and myself, not quite 9, to begin our very first paid job. We were strawberry pickers.

In order to get to the Duesenberry farm, we had to maneuver through a number of fields, and under or over a few electric fences. Eddie and a friend of his seemed to be able to get over the electric fences with no trouble at all. This amazed me, so I ask how they did this. They said that they simply built up a tolerance for electricity and then they suggested that I hold unto one of them while the one in front touched the fence. Do you know what? The person at the end gets the shock! What a fool I was. I am pretty sure the shock I got that day is what is turning my hair grey now.

We probably spent six hours a day in the fields. It was really quite usual for kids to work crops back then. We were joined by moms who needed extra money and even some high school kids who hadn't landed a better summer job.

Six hours in the fields seemed like eternity. We often had our lunches finished way before noon. This was long before strawberries had been engineered to be as big as they are now. It took forever to fill 6 boxes for a carrier worth 25 cents for labor, Since the strawberries we picked were going to be used to make jam, we picked by removing the stem so the juice covered our hands and arms until they were literally black by the end of season.

Crawling through that rich Washington soil also meant stained knees that took a bar of lava soap and a few good scrubbings to get off.

Of course, Eddie was one of the best pickers and I was sometimes encouraged er was that chastised by the field boss, to pick up my speed. Nonetheless, by the end of the season, I had a tidy little sum in my saving box. Still the summer wasn't over so we were sent down by the Nooksack River that bordered our property, to pick wild blackberries to sell in town. School was beginning to look pretty good and I could hardly wait for it to begin again.

By that summer, we were well entrenched in a little church called Ferndale Bethel. Mom and Dad taught Sunday school and we were learning more about the kind of people we should be now that we were a "Christian" family. Mom also read us countless stories at night from good Christian books like the Sugar Creek Gang and the Three Baers series. I took the message that we should be giving and sharing,

To end the summer, the church planned a big Labor Day picnic a week before school began. We met at a park in Birch Bay that had carnival rides on one side. I had brought my little box of money along with me.

Since, the other kids had not been as industrious as the McCay's had been that summer, we were the rich kids for that moment in time. I decided that the "Christian" thing to do was to share my riches, and in no time at all I was the benefactor of any kid who wanted to ride the Ferris wheel or the Merry-go-round one more time. It was a wonderful feeling, but it was fleeting. Someone ran and told mom and dad how nice I had been. They were not as impressed with my good deeds.

One the way home I got a good lecture about my wastefulness. Of 40 dollars of hard earned cash, I now had less than $10.00 left. It was only then that I learned mom and dad were counting on me to buy some of the nice things I wanted to wear to school. They were out of money. I was to get a spanking for what I had done.

Now, I am sure my spanking was more out of the frustration for my stupid deed than anything. I know how much they loved me and how sorry they were that I had ruined my own dream. It was the only spanking I really ever got from dad, but it was a lesson to remember.

While it is still so much fun to be able to provide enjoyment for others, I learned that day that we must also be prudent with our money. That was when I began my endless lists of grandma's money management I.e. budgeting. The more careful we are, and the more wisely we take care of our own needs, the more we will have to give. It was a lesson well learned and I AM GLAD.

Proverbs 21:20- There is desirable treasure, and oil in the dwelling of the wise, but a foolish man squanders it.

The Bible has much to say about taking care of the poor and much about good stewardship, but I think this verse in Proverbs says it best for my situation. When we wisely spend our own money, we will have more to give to help others. We also need to be wise in helping the less advantaged. What is better to give a poor person: a gift card for Starbucks or a gift card to a grocery store? Why? Think about it.

An Unforgettable Birthday Party

S chool was starting one week after our infamous Labor Day picnic and I was frantic. I had blown my hard earned 'berry money" on all the kids who either didn't have money, or who were too smart to spend their own cash on such frivolity as carnival rides. My fame was short lived and I was nearly broke. The $8.60 remaining would need to be used for socks and underwear. Dad would buy school shoes.

Ever since I had begun attending Ferndale Elementary in 3rd grade, I had envied the popular girls wearing the pretty dresses with generous swirl skirts, big puffed sleeves and those huge sashes that could be tied in giant bows.

To make matters worse, I was in a growing spurt. How was I even going to fit into last years' school clothes anyway? With all the work getting the farm working, building a new chicken coop, planting a garden, canning and preparing for our soon to arrive sibling, there had been no time for mom to sew or repair clothes either.

I am sure my mom was worrying about the same thing. That week she got out a box of used clothes that had been sent earlier in the summer from my older cousins, Loretta and Audrey, and she began to sort through them. There she found two perfectly good corduroy suits along with a black and white checkered skirt. I tried them on. I was sure I looked ridiculous. Mom was pleased.

Since Cousin Audrey was quite thin, all she would have to do was hem the sleeves and the skirts. Of course, there was nothing she could really do about the darts in the suit coats that were meant to accommodate the shape of a young women and most certainly not this soon to be 9 year old. In no time at all I was suited (pardon the pun) up for school.

Thinking back, I probably looked like Mary Poppins when I went out for recess to play jump rope. Yes, I did get teased from my peers. One boy started calling me Mrs. Gladys and then laughed his head off. The fact that several teachers complimented my attire didn't exactly make me feel better about my situation.

Anyway as I pondered my fate, I remembered that the really popular kids were always going to birthday parties. It seemed like every share and tell session, someone would recount all the fun they had at someone s birthday party. They played games like pin-the-tail-on the -donkey and giggled at the fun times they had had. Well, we didn't have a donkey and I doubted if dad would want us trying to do anything like that to the dairy cows, but I thought I could probably come up with something fun.

I had just turned 9 the week before school started so I asked mom if I could have a birthday party. Never mind that she was overdue with child. It had never stopped her from doing anything else. She told me to go ahead as long as I planned it. I suspect that she was thinking I would invite my best friend over to join our family. She was mistaken.

Now, I had never been to a real birthday party so I didn't realize there needed to be invitations, or perhaps a guest limit, so on the first day of school, while everyone was sharing all the fun they had had that summer, I marched up in my green corduroy suit and invited the entire class to my house for a birthday party after school the following day.

Now lest you think the entire class came, they did not. Apparently, the popular girls weren't going to get on a school bus and go to some weird farm girl's house. However, I did have a good friend from church named Rosalie who was allowed to come AND there were 5 or 6 boys, who were generally considered a little rowdy, who were all too happy for such an adventure.

Back in our day, it didn't take more than a note from home to take a school bus to someone else's house. Imagine my mother's chagrin when she saw that she had an extra 7 guests for the evening meal. The first thing she did was tell my brother Eddie to go out and kill 2 more chickens for dinner while she hastily made a birthday cake.

Of course, I didn't exactly have any specific plans so we went out to watch Eddie execute the chickens. A master at this chore, he skillfully put their heads on the chopping block and then with one swift ax beheaded them. Then he let them go! Do you have any idea what happened? A chicken has involuntary muscles and will actually hop away even though headless. The boys chased the headless chickens with glee and I cringe today thinking about their recounting of this task at later share and tells. Thankfully, it was years before PETA or we might have put that little dairy on the map right then.

After dunking the chickens in boiling water and plucking their feathers, mom took over and I led "the gang" into the little woods behind our home. First I cautioned them to be on the lookout for possible bears and cougars and warned them to be very quiet as we tip toed through the pine needles. I told them that a child had recently been attacked by a cougar, though I neglected to tell them that the incident had actually happened 150 miles away.

We visited a little fort that someone else had started and that had become a fun place for my brothers to work on the previous summer. I volunteered that it was likely a hideout for bank robbers or the like.

About that time a huge vulture decided to exchange its' residence by moving from one tree to another. Twilight was just setting in. My terrified guests took off like a shot of lightning and we were back at the dairy in no time at all.

Mom was still busy cooking dinner and when we came in she gave me "the look" so I knew she had no plans to entertain this bunch, and I had better get them off from under her feet while she finished the meal.

Off I went with my hapless entourage of party goers to our newly constructed chicken coop with a corrugated tin roof. The coop was built right next to the bull pen where our prize bull was kept. Of course he was also staked out, but any infringement on his territory would cause him to snort and paw the ground. This had caused the ground in the bull pen to become very fine powder consisting of rich dark Washington soil and lots of old manure. It also made a soft landing as would slide down the corrugated roof and jump into the bull pen, then quickly roll back under the electric fence to imagined safety.

Now it is doubtful that the bull could have ever pulled up stake and reached us, but this adventure left more than the aftermath of an adrenalin rush. It left the party goers covered from head to toe in a film of fine manure dust.

Later, we ventured to the haymow where Eddie had meticulously constructed a clubhouse for his friends while stacking the bales of hay that summer. There was a huge pulley that ran across the top of the haymow and out the haymow door. The men would send the hay bales up by pulley and Eddie would stack them. He cleverly built secret passages and his own clubhouse under tons of hay. This assured him the position of most creative and popular farm boy in the neighborhood until later that year when mom and dad noticed an unusual amount of activity in our barn and checked it out. Our horrified parents put an end to this dangerous venture then, but at the time of my party it was still intact. Luckily, all the fourth grade adventure seekers found their way out.

I doubt if our cows gave their usual supply of milk with the bunch of us terrorizing them that evening. We had milk machines which had to be moved from cow to cow. This fascinated the boys and they wanted to assist. Apparently the school hadn't thought to take these kids on a field trip to a dairy before. Poor dad He was having enough trouble trying to get the dairy running without my helpers.

The dairy barn was built on the side of a hill. Out the back door of the barn was a huge pile of cow manure. For sanitation reasons, the pile had to be quite a distance from the barn. Every night the manure was wheel barreled out to the end via a 2 by 12 plank way.

Since we were on the side of a hill, by the time the pile was reached we were actually quite high and could add to the pile from the top. Walking the plank took on a whole new meaning that night. Only sheer luck (and maybe some of dad's prayers) kept one of them from dropping off the end.

Finally, with the milking done, it was time for dinner and the birthday cake. I blew out my candles but there were no presents. Rosalie had given me a little sachet on my real birthday and apparently none of these boys had ever been to a birthday party before either, so the idea of presents had escaped them.

This was before seatbelt laws had been passed, so my exhausted mother crammed all the kids into our two seat Chevy and took them home. There was no room for me. By the time she got back, I was in bed and pretending to be fast asleep. I listened while she and dad discussed the whole evening and I decided that I wouldn't be planning any parties for a while.

Now if my birthday party did not grant me the popularity I wanted, it certainly gave me some notoriety. While some of these boys may not have been regulars on the share and tell circuit, they were all too happy to tell about my party. What I thought might be an ordinary day on the farm was immortalized by these thrill-seeking boys. I am sure the girls made a mental note to overlook any would be invitations, if sent from me in the future, and I am just as sure a few more boys wished they had been there.

No, I didn't get the party I had dreamed of, but do you know what? It was a party to remember and I imagine that it was the only party some of those boys, like myself, ever got invited to in grammar school. The last time I had a conversation with mom she brought up this ill-fated party. For all the memories and chuckles my family had over this misadventure, I AM GLAD.

Proverbs 15:13a A merry heart makes a cheerful countenance.

Some of the silliest things we do make the best memories. So what if things don't always turn out like we plan? It is better to laugh with the people who are laughing at you than to go and hide in embarrassment. This way you both get to enjoy the fun

The Preacher Man
brings big Changes

Fourth grade was an unforgettable year. We all joined 4H where my brothers dutifully learned how to take care of their animals and girls learned how to knit and embroider. At least, that was the plan. Eddie, as usual, shined in animal husbandry. His heifer even won grand champion at the county fair. On the other hand, my handiwork was simply too disgraceful to even be entered. Maybe, I would do better in canning next year—at least we could hope.

Little Rodney, McCay, baby number 6, joined the family just 2 weeks after my infamous birthday party. It was always fun to have a new baby in the house and he was the best natured little guy we could have ordered. Another baby hardly put a dent in the busy schedule of our farmer parents.

Sometime during the year, it was learned that a man was going to be coming to the Grange Hall and teaching Hawaiian guitar lessons every Friday. For some reason they could add more kids in for a reduced price. We, McCay's were always looking for these kinds of bargains. Of course, his plan was really to sell the more pricey electric Hawaiian steel guitars, but we could start on a big cheap wooden one. Well, mom knew we could never afford a piano, which was her dream, so she decided that at least we could get some culture with these affordable lessons.

The guitar lessons idea was all pretty exciting at first because most of our 4H friends were also going. Then, alas, we learned we were also expected to practice. Now mom and dad always anticipated the best out of us, so we weren't to lag on this either. However, it wasn't too long until 3 kids practicing Good Night Ladies on the wood guitar was just too much in our tiny little house. Mom requested that we take turns using the car outside to practice. How boring was that! Unfortunately, I managed to smuggle more than one library book out to the car to read during practice time. That, dear grandchildren, is no doubt the reason you do not hear me playing the Hawaiian guitar at our family gatherings!

One Friday we all arrived at our guitar lessons only to discover that our teacher had run off with his secretary, and taken all of the money parents had paid for the electric guitars with him, instead of turning it in to the company that had employed him. Well, that was an exciting turn of events. We now knew a real criminal and we would have a perfectly good excuse for stopping those dreaded lessons. I think our parents were just as relieved as we were. So much for culture.

Back in those days, before television was widespread, we felt very lucky to have an electric radio which sat on top of the refrigerator and gave us a constant update on news, weather, and local events. In addition, there was story hour from 5 to 6 where we could all listen to Sky King , The Green Hornet, The Royal Canadian Mounties, or Lassie. These 15 minute adventures were an amazing incentive to get our chores done and they were something all the kids could talk about on the bus. Some of the luckier kids even sent in for the enticing prizes offered on these shows like the genuine decoder rings (though I have no idea what needed to be decoded) or the flashlight that could beam up distress signals in event we got lost in the woods (or on the way to the outhouse) at night.

During those long rainy nights in the winter, we would play games or do hobbies around the kitchen table. I even taught dad to play jacks and he and I had some pretty spirited games. Of course with dad's big hands, we had to use a big rubber ball the size of a small baseball so my overall skill was not greatly enhanced. I remained the undisputed grand jack champion at the McCay residence only.

One day mom came into a plentiful supply of blue yarn. The idea was for me to take up knitting as so many of the other young ladies were doing. I learned a basic stitch at 4H which I, unfortunately, taught big brother Eddie. In no time at all, he was better than I. We made a game of knitting races and then we would tear out the yarn and start all over. That sorry experience is also why you have no lovely keepsake knitwear from your grandma.

My little space on my top bunk was my haven. There I read many books, did homework, and tried to learn how to sing from a church song book. Try as I might, it occurred to me and any one else that heard me, that I would never be a candidate for the choir. I think I got this message first, when my brothers from their side of the bedroom barrier complained of the noise. Sweet little Janice only 4 years younger, had a gift for music from her earliest years and while I howled, she could sing.

Of course, our life revolved very much around the church. We worked hard to learn verses and to get attendance pins. There were so many activities that were church based. There were missionary speakers from exciting foreign lands so I decided to become a missionary. There were revivals with stirring preachers so I repented of my sins on a regular basis. I loved church!

Christmas was amazing. I remember the first year we had an actual story of Christ's Birth played out. Some of the men wore their wife's chenille bathrobes to act the part of wise men and I recognized the gifts as vases from around the church. Somehow, old brown gunny sacks were used to make the lowly shepherd's garments and, of course, the tattered white sheets made great Angel costumes.

Nevertheless, it was wonderful to hear and see the Christmas story again. I remembered my disappointment with Santa Claus and I thought how much better the truth was I vowed I would never let Santa Claus take the place of the real Christmas Story.

Christmas was always a wonderful time at the McCay's. Mom made all kinds of homemade candy and dad made his famous popcorn balls. Somehow mom and dad always managed to afford something special for each of us. That year I got some genuine roller skates: the kind that adjusted to shoe sizes and had a key to tighten around the sole of the shoe. The only place to skate was our barn where there was an alley of cement behind the milk cows, which were firmly secured in their stalls. If I started to fall going around the corner, I would sometimes grab a cow's tail to keep from falling in the manure which was treated with lye. No wonder milk production was down!

I had a good friend to visit too. She also lived on a little farm a few miles away. When we wanted to get together, we would use the telephone. This meant picking up the phone and telling the operator who we wanted to speak too. She might even tell me to call later because Rosalie had gone to town. She knew everybody's business.

Many people were on the same farm line so it was very rude to stay on the phone for very long. Each home had a certain series of long and short rings to determine who should pick up, For instance, it could be a long a short and then 2 longs. Often we would run all the way to the house thinking we had a call and then find out it wasn't for us at all. However, with a little listening, it was also pretty easy to find out what the neighbors were up to! (now, of course grandma would never think to do something like that!)

Rosalie and I could spend a good Saturday afternoon exploring in the woods or playing in the many ponds. Once we found a nice size pond with a homemade wood raft and decided to take off for an adventure. We gleefully pushed the raft around the pond with a huge long stick that had been on the raft for this purpose. Then we dropped the stick. We couldn't reach the bottom of the pond and we couldn't swim. We laid down and tried to paddle the raft with our hands but it was way too heavy to budge and it remained stubbornly stuck in the middle of the pond. It was getting late and it was getting cold. No none knew where we were.

Since we both went to church together, we knew we had better pray about this one and that is exactly what we did. A wind came up and blew little waves on the pond. Our raft finally began to move and after while it landed in some reeds where it was much more shallow. We waded to shore. God heard our prayer didn't he? We never forgot that adventure.

One day we learned that our preacher was retiring and we would soon have a new pastor. This was a surprise. I wondered "who in the world could ever take the place of our kind, wise, elderly pastor"? I soon found out.

Somehow, mom and dad learned that our new pastor had a wife and 4 children, so as soon as he got there, they invited him over. While we didn't have much money, we always had plenty of food and mom and dad were very hospitable people. They truly enjoyed company.

Now Pastor Whitney had a big booming pastor voice. Back then we didn't use microphones so I always assumed that when God called someone to preach, he had to give them a preacher voice. Besides his preacher voice, he also had a singing voice like George Beverly Shay. He kept my attention. He seemed to know everything about the Bible and he told a lot of good stories. He even knew when the world would end and it was going to be pretty soon because everyone had become very wicked. I did my part to stop this ominous event. I repented again

Pastor Whitney and his family settled into the parsonage which was connected to our church. Some Sunday school classes were actually held in the bedrooms of the parsonage. Everyone used the parsonage bathroom. What a funny way to live, but that was normal back then.

Pastor Whitney and his family began to visit our home on a very regular basis. Since it was such a small house, and I often laid awake until very late, I would listen to their conversations. It seemed like some of the people in the church did not like this Godly man and they might not invite him to stay. I could hardly believe it! I thought these people were supposed to be Christians but instead they were mean. Maybe they should repent. No wonder the world was ending with people like that running the church. Of course, I didn't share this information with anyone because I wasn't supposed to know it, but it did affect how I viewed these church people.

Well, before the year was up, Pastor Whitney and his family had been asked to leave and they all moved to Oregon where they had family. We kept in touch and mom and I even went down once to visit them with our car packed with canned goods and things to help.

It wasn't long before my nosey ears began to pick up other information while I lay in that top bunk late at night. The dairy wasn't doing well. Dad had been sick twice with pneumonia and Eddie had had to practically take over during those times, Eddie was only in 7th grade. There were a lot of differences between a farm in North Dakota and a dairy in Washington. Maybe a dryer climate would be better for dad.

I began to worry about our future. By this time I had figured out that dad would probably never do anything but farming because that was all he knew. He was a VERY smart man but he had only been to school for 3 years in his life. So much for my Dick and Jane life — I just hoped we could save the dairy.

One day mom and dad had an announcement: we were selling out and moving to California! I was not happy. What would we ever do in California?

Since I always loved to talk, I didn't miss this opportunity to share the news at school. Oh my! My classmates were so jealous. Wasn't that were all the movie stars like Margaret O'Brien and Shirley Temple lived? Of course, I got all the mileage I could out of that bit of information, but I was secretly worried about what we would do when the money from the dairy ran out?

It turns out, that my parents had been in contact with Pastor Whitney, who was now at a little church in a town called Meiner's Oaks in California. We would be visiting him on the way to Long Beach where my Uncle George had a filling station. Dad, it seemed, could probably get a job there.

We loaded up our 1946 Chevy and hooked up the green trailer again. We packed up mom's canned goods along with the worn blue divan (sort of a futon which we used in the living room for a couch and for overnight guests), the dissembled bunk beds and our prize possession, an electric Frigidaire. Of course mom's homemade quilts and what few other linens we had were stuffed in between everything else.

We said goodbye to our friends and neighbors. We said goodbye to our relatives. We were off to the unknown. This time, I was the one crying.

Life does not always go like we plan. I have learned that God has a more certain plan for our life and often it is much later that we see how perfectly everything turns out, and for that lesson I AM GLAD.

Romans 8:28 And we know that all things work together for good to those who love God and are called according to his purpose.

Did my parents love God? Certainly! As you can see as you read the rest of the story—all things did work together. That is why you, my precious, grandchildren are here. I would never have met your grandpa if I had not moved to California.

Living Good at the Back of the Bus

We took our time getting to California because dad always liked to see attractions along the way. We might eat our meals in the park and cram way too many kids into a motel room, but we wouldn't miss the world's weirdest tree or the biggest gumball or any other thing that might enlarge our experience bank.

What a gift that was for us! Of course, we didn't appreciate all of this until years later. Now I know that enjoying the trip is often so much more important than getting to the destination.

I always remember once standing in line in Fort Yates, North Dakota and paying 10 cents to see a dead whale that had been trucked in from the East Coast. It stank so bad I thought I would vomit. Too bad Dad didn't know we would someday be able to visit Sea World and see some live ones up close or he might have passed on that one.

We never quite made it to Uncle George's in Long Beach. It turned out that Pastor Whitney and his family had taken up residence in a dumpy little apartment in Meiner's 'Oaks and they had located a similar residence for us in a little beach community called the Rincon, about 10 miles north of Ventura.

Pastor Whitney was now a pastor of a church in Meiner's Oaks about 25 miles away. However, they had found us a rental for a mere 15 dollars a month with only the train tracks and a major highway separating us from the beach. I was truly unappreciative of my beach experience.

I guess the church wasn't paying Pastor and his family much so they weren't eating too well either. Mom quickly began to unload our food and do what she did so well. She started making those amazing meals out of her canned goods and supplies. Soon she was baking homemade bread and conjuring up a good stew while the pastor and his family began to convince my dad that he should look for work around Meiner's Oaks because Long Beach was no place to raise kids. A tour of this ramshackle unpainted house we were living in made me wonder how Long Beach could be any worse.

Before long we were unpacking and planning to stay awhile. This was not good news! Is was bad enough to have to move to California, but did we have to find the most awful place still standing to live in while my parents checked out the area. Worse yet, my parents registered us for school in Ventura. I had visions of living the rest of my life there. I was in despair. Oh, how I missed Washington—outhouse and all. At least we had a barn to play in and we had our 4H and church friends,

By the following Monday, we were all boarding the school bus for Ventura. I was still wearing my corduroy suits, which actually fit me better by now than the year before. Nevertheless, I was also even more out of style in Ventura than Ferndale, I was doomed.

On the way to school, we went through an area that picked up several black kids. I was totally fascinated by them. Up until this time, I had rarely glimpsed a black except for the missionary slide shows from Africa.

They (the blacks) always marched to the back of the bus and seemed to have a great time together. There was no bullying, but there was also virtually no camaraderie between the whites and the blacks. They seemed to ignore each other as though the other group did not exist. Later I learned that in the Southern part of the United States, where these kids may have come from, blacks were forced to the back of the bus. Isn't that shameful? Maybe that is why they always stayed there.

I was a good student and it is easy to remain anonymous in a classroom, but recess was miserable. I had no friends to talk to or play with so I made my way to the tether ball line. I had never seen a tether ball before. I was awful at the game. I simply went up for my turn, got beat and then went to the back of the line to wait for my turn again. I kept wishing the bell would ring to end my loneliness.

One of the black girls from the bus was the undisputed tether ball champion. She was virtually unbeatable and seemed to love the role.

I guess my curiosity about these blacks caught me staring at them from my seat on the bus, and they took it as an offense. No matter where I sat it was always ahead of them, so one of them would manage to reach over and jerk my pigtails on the way off the bus. My misery was complete.

Now I really wanted to be a friend to these kids, or at least come to some sort of a truce. I remembered that missionaries went all the way to Africa to reach them for Jesus. They were certainly ignored here. Maybe, I could be a missionary to them. They would come to Jesus and we would all be friends. That seemed like a reasonable plan, don't you think?

One day, in my ignorance, I went to the back of the bus (well almost) and I said the unpardonable, "I don't know why you don't like me. I like you even if you are niggers," I did not get the opportunity to finish my little sermon. Even the black boys demanded I get back where I belonged.

I had made 2 big mistakes. I did not know that the term niggers was not acceptable and I had come off as being better than them. I was so ashamed. I deserved to have my pigtails jerked, but that day a funny thing happened. No one bothered to jerk my pigtails. It felt almost worse to be ignored. It made me understand how they must have often felt.

You can imagine how bewildered I was the next day when I got to the front of the tether ball line and the black girl stopped me before I began to play, and showed me a better way to serve the ball by holding it taut. I wondered why she would help me. Hadn't I blown it by my stupidity?

I actually began to play a little better. Later, she showed me how to position myself on the court. One day, to my own amazement, I managed to beat someone. She cheered! She acted like a friend and indeed she was.

Soon I became a formidable tether ball player and sometimes even kept the championship spot for a whole recess. I never excelled at sports but I was a pretty good at this game, thanks to my new black pal.

Another day and another miracle. I was actually invited to sit in the back of the bus with my new friends. When they got off the bus they told me to be sure to save them a seat the next day. Of course, no one else ever sat in the back of the bus anyway, so that was no problem. I had a mission and I took it seriously, especially since it also meant I would have someone to sit with too.

Every time my black friends got on the bus they acted as though I had done a great favor by saving these seats. We laughed and we joked. I was no longer anonymous. It made me feel so good to know that now I had a place with my new friends at the back of the bus.

My best memories of the end of 5th grade were the wonderful friendship and acceptance I felt with my black friends. They had forgiven my ignorance and cared for me anyway. I learned that great friends can be found in the most unusual places. Too often we look for people who are just like us when we might find better companionship and greater opportunities for growing if we sought out people who had different qualities and life experiences. For the lessons I learned and the incredible love I felt during this dark venture in my young life, I AM GLAD.

James 2: 1-20 tells us that we should never show partiality with people because of how their status in life is perceived. Who are we to ever judge another person's worthiness? We are to love everyone as we love ourselves, just as God loves and created us all.

In the end, it was those amazing black friends who took me in. It was they who chose not to judge or show partiality.

Granny Finds Cure for Depression

The summer between my 5th and 6th grade year, dad found a job at a small dairy on the outskirts of Meiner's Oaks. This soon sold to Royal Oak's Dairy near Ojai and it is there dad worked for the next 26 years.

As soon as dad had a job, they found a home at 216 North Poli in Meiner's Oaks. It had 3 bedrooms and, at last, an indoor bathroom. This was a quiet neighborhood (until we came) with several retirees and when they noticed our large family moving in, they started building fences. By the time we were settled, we also had a fenced yard.

Dad quickly added a large cement sport court/patio where we could play basketball, badminton, ping pong, or tether ball to our hearts content. That area was in constant use for almost 3 decades. Many childhood friends later recalled the parties they attended or the games they played there. It was the neighborhood hub.

We all went to that little church down the street where Pastor Whitney pastored. We soon got busy doing church stuff. Mom taught Sunday school and dad was the Sunday School Superintendent. We seldom missed a meeting, but trouble was brewing and I could feel it.

My penchant for nosiness coupled with lifelong sleep issues soon paid off. The pastor and his wife would often come to visit and after we went to bed I would hear them talking. Apparently, the same mean spirited kind of Christians that we had at our old Washington church went to our new church in Meiner"s Oaks. They didn't like Pastor Whitney either.

Soon Pastor Whitney was no longer the church pastor, He was going to do revival services and look for a new church with nicer people. Meanwhile, dad remodeled our garage (separated from the house) into a little 1 bedroom apartment the pastor and his family could use until things got better.

With my parent's good heart and the additional burden of 6 more people, our finances got worse. Dad was already working long hours at a poorly paying job so mom decided to go to work too. What she knew best was cooking, hence she took a number of restaurant jobs over the ensuing years. Our home became chaos.

As long as we had lived on a farm, we had had almost con-tinual access to our parents. Now they were often gone and instead the Whitney family spilled over into our house. I did not like to come into the kitchen and see Pastor Whitney and his wife drinking coffee and eating our food. They tried to exercise authority over us and I resented it. Had mom told them this was O.K.? I began to resent mom too. Hadn't she got us into this mess by befriending these users?

Sometimes Pastor Whitney would be gone. Sometimes he would take his wife and be gone. Mom would wind up feeding all of the kids after cooking all day somewhere else. When they were home, the kids mostly stayed outside, or at our house because pastor needed his time for study and prayer. I suspected he was sleeping and didn't want to be disturbed. I was certainly having my doubts about religious folks.

We, McCay's made great friends with our retired neighbors and soon we were doing odd jobs for them. Word got around that we kids would do just about anything for money and for less than anyone else. Before long, we had more jobs than we could handle and sometimes they were above our capacity.

I once got hired to do little retired ladies personal laundry. Since mom had always done our laundry and since I noticed mom always used a lot of starch, I decided it would probably be good to starch everything. When I left, her clothesline was lined with lingerie so stiff it looked like cardboard. I got 25 cents and she never called me back!

I took the bus to Ojai for 6th grade. Mom had gotten out our old treadle sewing machine and made me some nice California clothes for school out of an accumulation of flour sacks. Back then people used a lot of flour because it was cheaper to cook from scratch then use boxed goods, which were just coming out. Also, mom made all of our bread and that was a lot. Flour companies would compete by sacking their flour in a cheap grade of cotton with different patterns. We chose our flour by the design we liked.

There was a very nice girl named Pat Story who sat across from me. We practiced our spelling together and we both like to read. She lived in a tent while her dad was building their home, so she had a lot of stories to tell, I thought a tent might be a nice alternative to out bedlam at home since the arrival of the Whitney's.

When Pat's house was finally finished she invited me over to visit one Saturday. My amazing over worked mother managed to pull out a few flour sacks with a pattern that I just loved. There were pretty red cherries on a bright blue background. She made me a pair of culottes as a play set just for the occasion. I felt so special that day.

Pat took me on a tour of her brand new home. Then we got to the kitchen and I discovered that her mother had used the exact same flour sacks as my culottes for her dish towels. My secret was out! Pat's kind mother said she wished she had thought to make Pat such a nice outfit as I had, instead of wasting the sacks on dish towels. I secretly vowed to deep file my culottes and work very hard to earn enough money to buy a California wardrobe.

I am not sure exactly when my depression arrived but by the time school was out I was thoroughly depressed. I knew

I would never fit in anywhere. We, McCay's , were just mis-placed farmers and now we had this whole other family to take care of.

By this time mom was still working but planning to start a little restaurant in downtown Meiner's Oaks, besides all her responsibility for all these other people. Now, I don't know how she did it all so well, but back then I missed the time with mom and dad. Besides, I was going into a strange hormonal stage where my emotions surprised even me.

I didn't like a thing about California either. It was so brown. Even the mountains were brown. Having an indoor bathroom had lost its luster. All the California kids had televisions. Luckily, I had a lot of babysitting jobs so I knew all about I love Lucy and I Married Joan so I could pretend we had one too.

I began to detest the other people who had made themselves at home in our family. Maybe those church people were right when they let Pastor Whitney go.

One day when I just felt overwhelmed by all of my feelings I took a long walk alone. I sat on a guardrail that overlooked what we called the River Bottom. There was a steep cliff there and I began to wonder what would happen if I just jumped off?

Now I remembered enough from church to know this wasn't a very good option. Wouldn't my soul live on? How would I explain to my Heavenly Father how I had decided to take a life, even if it didn't seem to amount to much right then? Besides, the way my luck was going, I would probably just maim myself anyway. I wondered if anyone would even have the time to give me some sympathy. Ha! They probably wouldn't even notice I was gone.

Sitting there and watching the sunset, I began to think of any way I could change my situation. I know my mom was absolutely overwhelmed when she came home every Saturday to a messy house. She loved to keep a "good house". Tomorrow was Saturday. Maybe I could organize my wayward brothers into helping. After all, I was one of the "big kids".

I thought about all the times my parents had been there for us and how hard they tried. I thought about my brothers and sister. I loved them and they always made me laugh. We had had a lot of fun together. I had also found a little quiet library just 2 streets over that I could visit when things got too crazy at the McCay's.

As I began to think about what was right with my life and how I could fix some of what was wrong, an amazing thing happened. For the first time that summer I began to feel the depression begin to leave. I was on a mission. I was taking charge of my life. I was not going to keep blaming others for my problems.

The following day I organized the first surprise house cleaning for my mom. My brothers were not exactly thrilled, which is probably how I got the nickname, Sarge, but the effect was amazing. We cleaned, swept, and picked up, mopped and waxed all morning. When mom walked in the door, she practically fell over with joy. The feeling in our home was different that evening.

Now that I wasn't thinking just of myself, things began to get a whole lot better. I decided that I would do this again whenever I got the chance. I was still organizing these surprise house cleanings until the time I left home 6 years later. No wonder my brothers were so glad to see me go!

In an unexpected twist, my idea of going to the library when things got tough paid off. The library was a little tiny place. The elderly librarian lived in the back. She must have gotten some sort of a grant to run this little library in our small town and due to her age, it was becoming difficult. I spent so much time at the library, that she soon taught me how to check books out. I willingly filed all the incoming books. I had read most of them so I could also help people in making selections.

One day she offered to pay me. She didn't have very much money, she said, but she did have a nice working bike. She would sell it to me for $10.00 and I could work it off for 35 cents an hour. We had a deal!

By the end of the summer, I had an operational bike. I could go anywhere—well, anywhere a big heavy bike with wide tires and no gears could be peddled. I was thrilled.

I was also getting quite a few babysitting jobs in addition to helping mom at the restaurant and the week before seventh grade started, mom & dad took me to Ventura where I bought myself several nice store bought dresses for school. This time I actually (reluctantly) took the price tags off.

That summer, I had learned to take control of my own life and be thankful for what I had and I AM GLAD

Philippians 4:8—finally brethren, whatever things are true, whatever things are noble, whatever things are just, whatever things are pure, whatever things are lovely, whatever things are of good report, if there is any virtue and if there is anything praiseworthy—meditate on these things.

Psalms 100:4 Enter his gates with thanksgiving, and into his courts with praise…be thankful to him and bless his name. (NKJ)

James 4:17 Therefore, to him who knows to do good and does not do it, to him it is sin. (NKJ)

I will never downplay depression. It is a terrible place to be, but it is not hopeless, and incredibly the Bible does have the answers even though I must admit, I was not doing some sort of a spiritual search when I came upon the anecdote. It was only later that I realized my cure was exactly what the Bible ordered!

Depression has become a very popular diagnosis in this day and age. I noticed in an article several years ago that the first sign of depression is when a person is unusually focused on themselves. That is exactly what I was doing. When we get busy making someone else happy and when we stop blaming everyone else for our troubles, we will be on the road to recovery. Finally focusing on what is good in our lives and being thankful for what we do have will finish the task of healing.

Also...don't forget to call Grandma so I can remind you what a blest family we are!

Adventures of a California Tweenager

I turned 12 years old the same week I entered 7th grade at Nordhoff Junior High School. I was on a mission. Since it now appeared that I would be doomed to live in California until I was old enough to leave, I was determined to figure out how I could blend into this curious culture.

In Ojai Valley and feeding into our school were 2 little towns. One was Meiners Oaks where I lived and the other was Ojai. In between the 2 was an area known as the Arbolada. From my perspective, Meiner's Oaks was for the poorer people, like retirees and newlyweds. Ojai, which was actually an incorporated town, was for the middle class and the Arbolada was for the rich kids. Nordhoff High School and Junior High were located on one campus in the Arbolada area, so we all knew who came from the Arbolada.. Most of us suffered from a condition known as Arbolada Envy.

Back in our days, girls always dressed up for school. We never wore pants unless we were doing some sort of a club initiation, (which were commonplace back then.) I took note of a girl named Judy Meining from the Arbolada and noted what she wore. Her father was a dentist, one of those professional people I had supposed belonged to my old dreams of father in the Dick and Jane life. When she said she had bought some of her clothes at Jack Rose, it occurred to me I had better save quite a bit of money. Jack Rose was a lot pricier than the stores where we always shopped such as Montgomery Wards or Sears.

My very best friends came from Meiner's Oaks. They were Martha Smith, Jeanne Jones, and later Janice Cornine. We walked everywhere. If there was an after school event like a football game, we simply walked home afterwards. Football had to be played before dark anyway as like most schools then, there were no stadium lights.

Sometimes we just walked around town. There was Bink's pharmacy, Leggett's hardware store, Johnny's market, a dime store, a few smaller market's,, a yard goods store, and the Snack Shack, which was a popular hangout featuring hamburgers and malts and the good old Juke Box.

The Shack was the fun place to be, especially if we had some money for the Juke box, Since the only form of transporting music was by records, this was the way we could actually hear our favorites unless we were lucky enough to have our very own record player. (no doubt like the Arbolada kids).

There were no particular rules about how people had to keep their property back in Meiner's Oaks. We weren't in town very long until we learned about Miss Tuni's place. This was almost a city block of overgrown brush, random underground cellars, and a strange building in the center, with secret little hideaways, stairs that led to nowhere and doors that opened from the second story to a drop off on the outside.

Miss Tuni walked everywhere, chanting as she went, and when word was out that she was out of town, I am ashamed to say we sometimes sneaked on her property to try and discover the mystery of the whole complex. It was scarier than Freaky Friday. While the Ojai kids had their very own teen club and the Arbolada kids went to cotillion, we Meiner's Oaks kids had Miss Tuni's.

Mom's little restaurant closed after only a few months. With the Big and Middle kids in school, there was really no one to care for 3 year old Rodney with exception of the Whitney's when they were in town. One day, under questionable supervision, little Rodney decided to fix himself a snack by frying up our pet goldfish. This was just too much. Mom decided she was needed at home for the time being.

In the 50's, most families had only one car. It usually went with the wage earner to work, so it was very profitable to have small stores in walking distance and to have companies that delivered goods. The majority of people had fresh milk delivered daily. There was also the Helm's bakery to deliver bread and all kinds of bakery goods, the Watkins man for spices, jells and such, the Fuller brush man for cleaning needs, the Avon lady for toiletries, and the ice cream man were all mainstays in those days. Due to the McCay economy, we seldom took advantage of any of these conveniences. Mom continued to make almost all of our bread and churn our own butter. Dad had access to plenty of milk from the diary, especially if had been returned as too old to sell. Aged cream makes the best butter anyway and milk of questionable maturity could always be put into biscuits or pancakes.

Mom also continued to have a huge garden and nothing pleased her better than to have rows of her canned goods shelved on the back porch. I foolishly vowed to conduct my own life in a much more modern way. How I wish now that I had learned to garden and had gleaned some of the amazing skills I thought were too old fashioned then.

Remember the cement patio a.k.a. sport court dad had built? It was always busy with kids playing and when mom called us in for supper (that's what we called the evening meal) it often included whoever had been playing over Of course, supper might be just potato soup and homemade bread because money was always tight but between mom's garden and dad's dairy products, we were sure to have those things. Company was forever welcome.

Now I was always a competitive student, and back in 6th grade in a quest to learn how to read and understand music, all the 6th graders were required to take tonet lessons. The tonet is a cheap little wood instrument which is sort of a fore runner of a clarinet or saxophone minus any semblance of musical tone.

When the teacher told my mom how well I had done, mom was just sure I was musical, after all. Somehow, she and dad managed to scrap together enough money to make payments on a clarinet for me. I had no choice but to continue my musical journey into junior high. After all, we were still paying for that clarinet and my parents were unmoved in their opinion that I actually might have some musical ability. This meant I would be in Mr. Kaiser's orchestra//band, which was a rather sad little group of noisemakers garnered from both the junior high and the high school. I stayed in the band for the entire 6 years and the last time I played Pomp and Circumstance was at my own graduation.

While I eventually became 1st chair 1st clarinet, I assume it was more of a reward for my tenacity than talent. Still, we had a lot of fun with this odd combination of students. Mr. Kaiser was either a very patient man or he was totally tone deaf.

One day, Mr. Kaiser got the idea that we should put on a performance for the outside world. He would have both the orchestra and the choir do some sort of a spring concert. I wondered why.

Anyway, the week of the concert we were all told to all wear a dark skirt or pants and a white blouse. Well, I thought "at least we would look good". The problem was I had neither a white blouse nor a suitable skirt. My babysitting cache had already been spent (partly at the juke box). When I confided this to mom, we pooled our resources and bought 4 yards of cheap navy blue cloth and 2 yards of white material from the little dry goods store downtown. The cost was 25 cents per yard. We had an investment of less than $2.00. When I went to bed that night, mom was busy sewing on the treadle. When I got up the next morning, I had a brand new outfit! I had such an amazing mother.

Back in those days all the girls took a semester of sewing and a semester of cooking. Our teacher, Mrs. Wentworth, was responsible to be sure we could all run a home someday. Meanwhile, the boys were over in woodshop making knick knack shelves and maiming themselves. I'm sure the whole idea of classes especially designed for the specific sexes would be considered stereotyping today, but back then I think it made us feel special and gave us a certain mystic.

Gym was a whole new experience. All the girls were expected to buy white shorts and white blouses and we were graded partially on how clean and fresh we looked every Monday. This was before the introduction of polyester or any of the blended wrinkle free materials. A clean uniform for gym was one thing I could do and no matter how poor my abilities were on the volleyball court, I was freshly starched and ironed on the first day of the school week.

At one point I had apparently garnered enough friends to be chosen as short stop for the girl's baseball team. Instead of being thrilled, I was terrified. I had never played the game and I was just sure I would muff the first ball that ever came to me.

When I confided this to an elderly neighbor, whose house I periodically cleaned, she took matters into her own hands.

The next day Mrs. Smith's husband, Mr. Smith and their neighbor Mr. Matter, who were both very elderly informed me that they were going to teach me to catch and throw. I made a mental note to keep my mouth shut in the future.

Every night we stood on the street playing 3 corner catch. I was amazed that a ball thrown so slow could keep from dropping to the ground mid-air. No, I did not become a baseball whiz, but I still remember how much they seemed to enjoy the thought that they were helping me. Just a few years before the neighbors had resented our arrival and now they encouraged and supported us.

We developed special friendships with those older people over the years. They remembered special occasions and they cared about us. Now that we are the old people in the neighborhood, I hope that our little neighborhood kids will know that we care about them too. Age is no barrier to friendship.

As far as my faith, I must say it was faltering, at best. For some reason, when Pastor Whitney was dismissed from his pastor position at the church it affected our family too. We stayed when the new pastor came and we liked him but he had his own personal problems and an affair ended his marriage and position at the church. I was beginning to have a very dim view of all these hypocrites.

One day a man came to our home saying that he was starting a church in a tent in Oak View. He ask us to attend, He drove a bus all over and picked up people for church and then he taught Sunday school after which his wife led the singing and he preached. All the stress of the busy Sunday morning did not dampen his enthusiasm for preaching. He could easily go on well into the afternoon. Much to my dismay, my parents decided to give this church a try too.

Our new church, Oak View Full Gospel became a church home for us for over 20 years. It thrived. My parents thrived. This time I was a lot more reluctant to embrace the church. So while my parents taught Sunday school, helped build the new church and served in every way possible, my shaky faith became a matter of concern for them. Whenever the dear saints of the church warmly welcomed me by name, I was justifiably certain that it was because they had heard prayers on my behalf.

By the end of the school year, even I noticed that California had some real positives. We were 13 miles from the beach. The weather was more often nice than not. Friendships were being forged and, of course, we had the most important item: we had an indoor bathroom!

For the difficult times that make us appreciate better times and for the friends from every age, be it the church saints, the elderly neighbors or dear Martha, Jeanne, & Janice, I AM GLAD.

Proverbs 17:17 A friend loves at all times

Proverbs 18:24 A man who has friends, must himself be friendly.

Friend's come in many shapes, sizes, and ages. Don't over-look the value of older friends who can mentor you, or younger friends that you can mentor. Be a true friend. Do not gossip, envy, or use your friends for your own status in life. Be the kind of friend you would want to have.

Ship of Good Fortune
Docks in Ojai

About the time 7th grade ended mom went to work again. With lots of McCay kids out for summer, there should be no real problem with the middle and big kids available to take care of the little kids. We needed the money.

Now in our McCay family, everyone had jobs and plenty of them. Our phone rang like the employment office. Would one of us come over to trim the roses, or sweep off a roof or clean up a mess, or baby sit for a co-op? (Parents often joined friends to put their kids together to save on babysitting monies). We were available and the word was out. In fact, I used to wonder why the Whitney family had not heard of this marvelous idea. The job market was certainly open if anyone was willing to be the lowest bidder. We were.

Mom's new job was at a place called Wheeler Hot Springs. It was located up in the mountains about 5 or 6 miles away. There was a little diner located on highway 33 that fronted the rest of the resort, Mom could run this diner for the breakfast hour meaning she would be both the cook and the waitress. She offered me the job of being her waitress. I wasn't on the payroll but I could keep any tips I received.

Mom kept the café open from 7:00 to 11:00 but we had to be there to set up around 6:00. We could be home by 11:00 which was perfect for mom. I was there 2 days and the on-site masseuse offered me a job from 11:00 to 7:00 at 35 cents per hour as his receptionist. I could hardly believe my good fortune. I would have plenty of money to shop for school at Jack Rose this year!

I saw my very first movie star one morning in the little café. Doris Day and her mother came in. I was surprised to see that Doris had a lot of freckles but she was still very pretty and so nice. I could hardly wait to let my out of state cousins in on this. Maybe California would pay off after all!

My receptionist work was in a big old rickety building next to a warm sulfur pool which was open to the public. Very few people in those days had their own swimming pool so the pool was a very popular place for the local teens. A loud speaker system played all the popular music all afternoon.

What an exciting afternoon to be able to tan at the pool listening to Rosemary Clooney croon If you loved me half as much as I loved you or Patti Page singing How much is that Doggie in the Window? Of course, I was busy scheduling sulfur baths and massage therapy for the elderly next door, but I had my dreams.

One day a very interesting thing happened. The pretty life-guard next door came over and asked if I would cover for her while she took a break. My immediate thought was one of grave remorse. I could not swim. Mom had signed me up for swimming lessons after we came to California but I had been put in a class of kids 3 years younger and I was too prideful to continue. I confessed my problem, but was assured that nothing bad could possibly happen anyway. There were too many people in the pool for a drowning soul not to be rescued by someone nearby. That was good enough for me. For the rest of the summer I strutted around the pool with a whistle any time a break was needed. I shudder to think what may have happened.

By the end of the summer I had accumulated over $400.00. Jack Rose was just waiting for me. Dad had other plans for my newfound wealth. He mentioned that that amount of money was actually more than he made in an entire month. It might be wise to save some of it in case my situation changed. He suggested half. I was dumbfounded, but when he assured me the bank would take good care of it and I could always get it out when needed I reluctantly relented. I still had ample for some nice school clothes. Within a few years, I had enough money to buy my first car with plenty left over and it really hadn't hurt that much.

I learned something in the way of saving. Just like Joseph had taught the Egyptians back in Bible times, it is always good money management to save in times of prosperity because lean years will come. I watched how prudently mom and dad consistently lived and yet we always had enough to help others or do the important things in life. For the example they provided in handling financial matters, I AM GLAD.

Matthew 25:27- Therefore you ought to have deposited my money with the bankers— —(NKJ)

Well, Grandma is certainly cheating to use that verse. Look up the story. I think the best example is the story of Joseph who saved Egypt by saving in times of prosperity for the lean times ahead. That wonderful story starts in Genesis chapter 40. We are in an economic downturn right now. Sadly, some of the people who made very good money when the economy was doing great did not save any of it. Now they have to sell their boats and Jet Ski's for a pittance so that they can barely live. Be careful in the good times. Know that bad times usually follow. Be prepared.

Sometimes Life just isn't Fair

S ometime during my Junior High years I realized I knew just about everything. Well, at least I had an opinion on just about everything. Imagine my surprise, one day, when mom was having a rather heated discussion with one of my brothers, and I chimed in to "help" mom understand the facts and she slapped me hard! I was stunned. After all, I was just trying to assist in resolving the matter.

Now, please understand that a slap was hardly considered child abuse in those days, so calling the child abuse hotline was out of the question. There was no such thing anyway. However, I had seldom been slapped and my last spanking at age 9 was the time I misspent all my hard earned money entertaining everyone I knew at the carnival.

I was wounded, embarrassed and angry. I slunk to my bedroom and locked the door. Apparently all the stress of working and trying to raise all of us had caused mom to snap, but that was no excuse. I vowed to stay out of her reach and her life forevermore.

Mom would be sorry when I no longer surprised her by organizing the troops to clean house. I would stay in my room until I was old enough to leave home. Well, I might have to go out to take a phone call, or a bathroom break, or babysitting job or school, but aside from that, they would never see my face again. Of course, I would have to let Janice in, because we shared a room. Maybe I could get her to smuggle some cookies and stuff in.

I sulked in my room for a while and then mom started knocking softly on my door. She wanted to talk. I refused. She had had her chance and it was too late. I had no plans to forgive her. I might not even let my kids meet their grandmother, if I ever had kids, that is.

I listened smugly while my sister and brothers discussed my absence. They missed me. I hope mom was satisfied with what she had done to our family!

The following day, I repeated my behavior. I simply answered yes or no to any questions and retreated to my room again. Mom was beside herself. I was getting even (and a little lonesome) as I sat in my room by myself.

Ashamedly, I determined to repeat my behavior on the third day, but as I listened for my siblings to mourn my presence, a strange thing happened. They had stopped asking about me. My absence was the new normal. Hierarchy in the family was changing. Good grief, I wondered, were they going to forget about my grave injustice so soon?

Then it occurred to me that if I didn't get out and reestablish myself, I could lose my place altogether. I got up and marched out like nothing had ever happened but something had happened, and that was that I had learned a very valuable lesson. Everyone gets hurt sometimes, and life is not always fair, but we need to dust ourselves off and get back in the struggle or we will lose our place.

Yes, I was hurt again and you will be hurt too. Life will "slap" us all at some time. Sulking and blaming and retreating is not the answer. Get up and get on with living. That day, and many other times since, I have learned that forgiveness will only work when we put the actions of others behind us and press on, and for that lesson I AM GLAD.

Philippians 3:13b-14 forgetting those things which are behind and reaching forward to the things ahead, I press toward the goal for the prize of the upward call of God in Christ Jesus.

Grandma Takes up Crime

By 8th grade things were looking up. I was actually getting the hang of being a California kid. For the first time in my life, my wardrobe consisted mostly of store bought clothes instead of hand me downs, homemade, or made over attire. I had a collection of wool skirts and sweaters including one cashmere sweater that had cost a whopping $25.00. I considered that success in my shallow mind.

I was beginning to feel at home in my new church too, though I was certainly wary of getting too involved. I had a friend at church named Beverly who was as sweet and talented as could be. I think my parents may have wished I was a little more like Beverly and a little less like Gladys.

The Whitney's became less a part of our lives and soon they divorced in a little scandal that seemed to shock my parents, but was just what I was beginning to expect of so called religious people. I was starting to wonder a whole lot about religion and the phony's who seemed to use it for their own gain. I wondered if I would even go to church when I was out of the McCay home.

I pondered why mom and dad could so easily love and accept these people. Hadn't they been burned enough?

Our church was growing though, and mom and dad loved to entertain these people. Soon there were barbeques on the patio and young people's parties. I liked the party idea and whenever our Sunday school teacher promised a trip or a party for inviting people, I was all for it. I invited plenty of kids though my motives were questionable at best.

At Oak View Full Gospel Lighthouse, everyone called everyone else sister and brother because the Bible says we are all sisters and brothers in Christ. I had a little too much pride for that one. I remember once being with some friends in downtown Ojai and running into a church lady, who, being of large girth, no makeup, and a stained work dress, simply failed to meet my criteria of an acceptable sister. She, in turn, hailed me like I was a lost soul returned to the fold. That took some explaining and I doubt I made a bit of sense. Too bad I was so prideful. She truly was a sister in Christ.

Since the Junior High and High School shared both a campus and many facilities, we had many like goals and experiences. In fact, we also had the privilege of voting for the student body officers. That is how grandpa first came to my attention. He was running for the office of president (which he got). I did not vote for him. I thought he was just a little too bossy. Can you believe that?

Sometime in the spring or early summer of that year, Jeanne and I decided to take the bus to Ventura and go to the beach. The cost of a bus ride was 35 cents. The Greyhound bus station was near the beach. We were all set to get a great tan. I packed our belongings in a little beach satchel I had and off we went.

Unfortunately, we had no such thing as a weather channel back then. In fact, the McCay's still didn't even own a T.V. anyway, so regardless, we did not realize that the beach would be socked in with fog.

While waiting for the beach to clear, we decided to go to downtown Ventura and window shop. It was cold there too. Soon so we took refuge in the department stores and began trying on bathing suits. Nobody seemed to pay any attention to us. In fact, there wasn't a clerk in sight in the Montgomery Ward store we first visited. I found the cutest little green bathing suit for $5.98. I had enough money to buy it. Instead I put it in my satchel and walked out of the store. Oh My! This was just too easy. After a while we went down to Penny's Department Store and I did the same thing. This time it was a blue bathing suit for $4.98.

WOW, I thought. No wonder people steal. I would have to do about 30 hours of babysitting for the Wilson tribe to come up with that much money. (the last time I babysat those 4 little scoundrels, they had tried to start a fire in the bedroom) I pondered my savings but at the same time a very big heaviness came over me.

Well, we took our loot down to the Greyhound bus station and changed into our new attire. We really looked pretty good and the sun was out at last. Why then did it seem like it was still overcast? All the way home I thought about what I had done. McCay's would never steal no matter how bad things were. What a disgrace I was. What did Jeanne think of me? Worse yet—what did God think of me?

Now I had 2 choices to make. I could continue to steal because it was really pretty easy, or I could decide I would not be a thief and I would make what I had done right. I chose the latter and I never stole again. The problem now was how to make it right? I thought about sending the money to the stores anonymously but wouldn't that be a cop out? Maybe I deserved to be arrested. I had heard our pastor, who we called—you guessed it—Brother Mac, say that we needed to face up and make restitution whenever we did something wrong. That was filed away in my little brain.

Now I am going to jump ahead 6 years and tell you what I finally did. After I had married grandpa and after Aunt Susie was born, I still knew I had never made restitution for what I had done. My dad had found an old stroller at the dump which he gave to me for Susie. I had a little part-time job at the bank so I had some money. I decided to go to Ventura one day and confess what I had done at both stores and pay back what I owed plus whatever they thought was fair. Of course, I would need to take Susie with me.

Oh how I wished I had never stolen a thing. How hard it is to face up to a mistake that should have never happened. There is no worse misery than to have a problem you, yourself, created.

The first stop made was to JC Penny's. I found the manager on the first floor. He was quite amazed that I was paying for a bathing suit I had stolen years before. He thanked me and stuck the money in his pocket (hopefully to turn it in later.)

My next stop was Montgomery Ward. This was not so easy. The manager was in his office upstairs. I had to somehow carry Susie and the rickety stroller up the stairs without dropping her out. This was no simple task as no one had thought of belts for strollers yet. Finally I managed this undertaking and made my way to the back of the store with my noisy stroller going clickety clack all the way. Everyone was watching me. At the back of the store the billing clerks sat in a penned in area with the manager's office behind.

I told my story to one of the clerks. She turned around and yelled, "This lady stole a bathing suit. She needs to see the manager". I was so embarrassed as I made my way noisily through the office area to the manager's private domain. I was attracting even more attention. They must have thought that I had been caught red-handed.

The Montgomery Ward manager was a formidable looking character and he gave me no slack. I was sure he was going to have me arrested right there. I would probably be on the front page of the Star Free Press. What would I do with Susie? He told me the statistics on how much stealing costs stores. Finally, he ask why I had decided to come in and confess. I told him how much it had bothered me all those years and how I had been taught better. I told them that I was now a Christian and knew I had to make it right. Finally, he pulled out a Bible he had, and he told me he was a Christian too. He wondered if he could use my story in Sunday School. Of course, I said yes! When I walked out of that store it felt like a ton of bricks had been lifted.

Once I saw a story on Oprah about a rich lady who had a problem stealing and how she was in therapy for it. I wished I could have told her that the best therapy ever is to march right back and confess what you have done and pay it back. Your addiction will stop in its tracks and the right people will be getting your money. What a lesson I learned over this event. I learned that doing wrong may seem easy, and doing right is often hard, but it is always worth it to do the right thing and I AM GLAD.

Proverbs 22:1 A good name is to be chosen rather than great riches, and favor is better than silver or gold.

1st John 2: 3-5 Now by this we know that we know Him, if we keep his commandments. He who says "I know Him" and does not keep His commandments is a liar and the truth is not in him. But whoever keeps His word, truly the love of God is perfected in him.

By this we know that we are in Him.

If you truly love God, you will want to keep his commandments. If you ever find that you are breaking God's commandments and you have begun to justify your sin, you are treading on very dangerous ground. Take time to re-read the entire book of 1st John.

Grandma Under Falsie Pretenses

I was thirteen years old when it occurred to be that I needed a more shapely body. Scanning over movie magazines I scoured while babysitting some very late hours, I realized that I was built nothing like Marilyn Monroe or Elizabeth Taylor. I was almost 14. Surely, I should have morphed into something resembling a young lady by now. Did I really look like a teen-ager? Would I even fit in at High School this coming fall?

Now keep in mind that back in my day, surgery to alter the shape of one's body was unheard of, and would have been out of the question even if it was a possibility.

I pondered my situation for a while and then it occurred to me. At our little Meiner's Oaks' dime store, I had noticed a rather large quantity of rubber like appliances that women must be using for size enhancement. I wondered how these would work on me. I also wondered how I would manage to sneak these by mom.

Anyway, I decided that the situation was desperate and for 59 cents I was able to acquire a pair that would greatly change. my shape. Later, trying them on, it occurred to me that my future would be forever altered. Who knows? I might even be discovered by some movie producer, as this seemed to be the foremost criteria that most of them were looking for. Didn't I read that that was how Lana Turner was discovered?

I tucked my new found body shape alternators A.K.A. falsies in my beach satchel with my recently acquired green bathing suit. I was set. Now for a place to try them out. A few days later mom agreed to drive Jeanne and I up to Wheeler's Gorge for an afternoon swim. This was perfect. There were always loads of teens from our own area and from Ventura there. I would at least look like one of them now.

As soon as we went into the bathhouse to dress, I slipped by rubber devices into the top of suit. Well, it certainly did the trick. I was a changed young lady!

Now as I told you before, I really didn't swim because I had quit swimming lessons when I was too prideful to continue with kids much younger BUT thankfully I had stayed long enough to learn to float. Floating was O.K. because I figured I could also get a nice tan at the same time. I had no sunglasses so there I floated around with my eyes shut just imagining what a stunning figure I must be making.

Suddenly I noticed a funny tickling feeling on my upper arm. Was Jeanne trying to get my attention? I opened my eyes and saw no one. Then a sickening feeling came over me.

Perhaps part of my phony body had floated out. Sure enough, that was what it was. I grabbed it and came to my feet. Oh no, the other one was missing too! Here I was holding one and there was the other floating out of my reach. I couldn't deny they were mine because I was clutching the matching part. Its' twin was now too far for me to get to and everyone was trying to assist me as it bobbed further and further away. Finally a daring young kid actually managed to retrieve it. I could barely thank him as climbed out of the pool to hide in the bath house until Mom could pick us up. I had certainly gotten recognition, but not exactly for the reasons I wanted.

How I wish that was the last foolish or prideful thing I ever did, but what I learned is that it is better to laugh at ourselves than to try to hide who we really are. And for that I AM GLAD.

Proverbs 17:22 A merry heart does good like medicine.

Another Party Flop

Somehow, though we never had a television, every summer we s managed to take a vacation to see our relatives in either Washington or North Dakota, Family was everything to dad and mom. In fact, visitors who could claim the slightest relationship were always warmly welcomed to our abode. Sometimes, I suspected they just wanted to use our place as a motel while they saw the California sights.

Our vacations always started the same way. Dad would pack the car intending to leave bright and early the next morning and then would decide to get an early start and leave that night. McCay's were early everywhere we went, which is a curse I have success- fully overcome. (Maybe too success- fully according to your grand-pa), Often the excitement and hard driving would cause us to get to a place as much as a day ahead. The sheets intended for our bedding would still be wet on the line and our flustered hostess would be scrambling to put a meal together.

We never had more than a 2 seat car and air conditioning had not even been thought of. Cars had a little wind wing that could be opened for fresh air. When the temperature is over 100%, that air felt more like a furnace blast than a cooling fan.

We packed in like sardines and it was always a blessing for mom and dad when they could drive all night and save the cost of a motel. My ability to talk non-stop was put to good use on those nights. I got to sit up in the middle of the front seat and talk to keep dad awake while he drove. This meant mom could get a little sleep. Days, of course, dad looked for opportunities for us to see tourist highlights and get out of the crammed car.

Cars are made much better today than back then. We often had breakdowns, which is perhaps why dad wanted to get that head start. More than once a kind mid-west farmer would come upon us in a bad situation and spend a good part of his day helping dad bale the car back together so we could get going. How thankful we were to meet people with such good hearts. I hope someday, someone will think the same of us.

Just before ninth grade started, we finished a trip to North Dakota. I could hardly wait to get home and see Martha and Jeanne and Janice. California really was feeling like home. Somehow, the visits to the farms where my cousins lived were beginning to seem foreign to me. I never was much of a horse-back rider and the flypaper that hung above my aunt's kitchen table or the lack of hot water made me even more thankful for Meiners Oaks' city life.

Besides, North Dakota always greeted us with a frightening electrical storm and I did not want to face my maker before I had made amends for my bathing suit thievery.

School started and I loved it. The boys who had (wisely) totally ignored us as 8th graders, began calling like we had passed some invisible barrier to another world. Now, when Martha, Jeanne, and I would walk around Meiner's Oaks, the Ojai boys would cruise over to Meiner's Oaks and hoot and holler out of their cars at us while we pretended to be totally uninterested. Of course, we loved the new attention and all that walking was surely good to keep us in shape.

One fall day I was walking home from Bink's pharmacy when a very cute freshman boy named David Baugh rode his bike up and started talking to me. I was tongue tied for the first time in my life.

David was a freshman football player and he was wearing a miniature pewter football on a chain around his neck. As he talked he took the chain off and began to sort of toss it around. Then he dropped it. When he didn't pick it up I reached down to do so and he said, "You can keep it" and rode off. Wow—I had noticed other girls going steady wore their boyfriends football. Did that mean we were going steady? I called Jeanne and Martha and they both thought it did. I couldn't wait to get to school the next day and proudly wear my football.

I was a high school freshmen and somebody liked me. Of course we couldn't really date as he had no car and was too young to drive anyway.

I began to take stalk of my situation. My brothers had taken up taxidermy. It was not unusual for kids to go hunting in the river bottom and they had decided some of their treasures should be stuffed for the future. A strange assortment of birds (hopefully not on the endangered species list) hung to dry in the big oak that shaded our sport court. I would like to welcome my new boyfriend over, but when the wind took a turn, the dead bird stench left some explaining to do.

Finally, one Friday night David did came over. He didn't have a t.v. and neither did we, but I brought him into the living room away from the nesting dead birds in our tree. I found a radio with a ballgame on for him to listen to and mom evacuated the little kids out of the living room -or at least that was the plan. Mom was going to bake us some cookies.

As I sat on the couch trying to think of something clever to say, I noticed a gently mist coming down over us. My little brothers had taken flour and straws and had crawled behind the couch and were blowing flour into the air and on us. I was too embarrassed to tell David what was happening, but by the time he left, he looked like an ad for dandruff shampoo. So much for that first date! I would need to polish up those little urchins or forget bringing another boy home.

Mom and dad never left us and for good reason, so I was surprised one day when dad ask if I thought I could manage the family while he took mom on a little trip for their 20th wedding anniversary. Of course, the wheels were already turning. I checked with Martha and Jeanne and we decided it would be a good time to have a party. Maybe I could impress David too. Now mom and dad didn't forbid parties, and dad could be a real cut up BUT we wanted to have a grown up party. After all, we were 14!

There was sort of a loyalty code in our family, so I knew that unless the house burned down, no one would tell dad and mom.

We set about inviting everyone we knew, including a pretty new girl named Charlene from the Arbolada. I guess she didn't know a lot of people yet and she said she would come. Things were looking up.

We planned games and refreshments, but the party got out of hand when someone suggested spin the bottle. Now this can be a funny game with an adult around. A person is chosen to spin the bottle and they get to say what the person who the bottle lands on has to do like crow like a rooster. However with no adult, the idea of turning it into kissing game came up and I went along with it.

Nothing terrible happened. There was no drinking. There were no cops breaking up the party, but the party wasn't fun like I had hoped. Everything became awkward. I was so embarrassed that I managed to forget the whole thing for many years. It was only recently that Charlene reminded me of the party. Your friends will never forget the stupid things you do, so keep that in mind!

In my heart I knew that I had violated my parents trust. Actually the party could have gone quite well if mom and dad had been there. I was reminded again that day how important it is to honor our parents and I AM GLAD.

Deuteronomy 5:16- Honor your father and mother as the Lord your God has commanded you that your days may be long and that it may be well with you..........

Shortcut to Success

B ack in the fifties, board games were a very popular way to spend a long evening. T.V. was limited and not everyone had one. Activities had to be planned by us and not for us. During rainy cold winter nights Jeannie and I would sometimes play Monopoly with her older brothers and assorted friends.

Now if you have never played Monopoly, it is a game about life situations which are not always predictable and how to succeed in life. You role dice and where you land determines your fate. You could go to jail or you could have the opportunity to buy the space you land on and then charge rent to anyone else who lands there. Everyone starts with some money and you try to increase your fortune by not landing on the wrong space and buying the right space like life, some spaces (real estate) represented more and some less so you hoped you had made good decisions.

Jeannie and I were equally bad investors and lost way more often than we ever won. Of course, this evoked a lot of teasing and I suspect was a good reason her brothers were willing to play with us anyway. They could pretty much count on being winners.

One day when Jeannie was at my house we decided to borrow the money from the Monopoly set my brother had gotten for Christmas and take it to play with her brothers as a joke. We decided that with the extra money we would be sure to win the next monopoly game and turn the tables on them.

It wasn't long before our opportunity came and we were ready having stuffed our pockets with the phony cash. It was a little tricky smuggling the money to the table whenever we needed it but we managed.

Well, sadly we did not win the game even then. It just took us longer to lose.

Now we had to retrieve our money and admit we were big losers even with the borrowed money. Of course we really got teased after this episode, but I learned a lesson then. Sometimes we think we could play the game of life better if only we came from a richer family, had more connections, were more attractive or perhaps, in our case, a little smarter. The truth is, that it's not what we come in with that counts but what we do with what we have. For this lesson I AM GLAD

The Bible talks about this very thing. In Matthew 25:25 Jesus tells us of a wicked and lazy servant who only had one talent so he buried it instead of putting it to use. Whatever talent we are given, we are expected to use.

Who Rocked My Boat?

If you ever saw a re-run of Happy Days, you might wish you lived back in the 50's. Life was more innocent. People were more ethical. The tawdry was the exception, rather than the rule. Still, we had some serious concerns too. Russia now had the atomic bomb and they were threatening to destroy us. We were practicing on a bigger bomb called a hydrogen bomb so that if they destroyed us, we could always get even by wiping them out along with the rest of the world for good measure.

Sometimes, a very eerie cloud cover would form over Southern California. Everyone said this was from our bomb testing in the Pacific. Some people built bomb shelters to hide in in case we got bombed.

T.V. programs, like I Led Three Lives, highlighted the evil Communism perpetrated and how malicious our cold war enemies were. Since all of us could still remember World War II and some were still mourning the loss of family or friends in that war, there was always a certain fear lingering in the back of our minds as to what would become of all of us if we went to war again.

Every generation confronts pain and evil on some level. We will always be faced with standing up for what is right and sacrificing, even to death, so that others might enjoy freedom. Liberty and the right to worship freely.

With that in mind, I will tell you that high school was a wonderful time for me, but I also waged a war in my mind about the viability of the future and what my role would be. My faith was shaky. My trust was gone. I had lost that peace that had come when my father had accepted Christ in his life and we had begun on our journey as a Christian family. Now I wondered if my parents had been tricked and those old fears from my early childhood came back.

If my parents (and Brother Mac) were right, was I walking down a very dangerous path away from God's love and plan for my life? If they were wrong, what about all I would be giving up for nothing? (Not that I had much to give up–but just in case). What if God wanted me to be a missionary?

The Bible says that if we are ashamed of Jesus, he would be ashamed of us too. I invited people to church but was I really ashamed of Jesus? Look how embarrassed I had been when the shabby lady had called me sister in front of my friends? She was really a very kind lady. Would Jesus be ashamed of me for the way had acted?

Like most of us do when we don't want to make a decision, I tucked my fears and questions away and went on with my life.

I was a good student, so I was in the classes with kids who were generally from more successful homes. Anyway, homes that I defined as successful.

My steady boyfriend did not last long. Some girl told me he wanted to break up so without checking the story out, I simply went over and tossed his football back at him in front of his friends. My, what a mature thinker I was! He moved that year and three years later he called for a date. I went out just for curiosity and you guessed it! He said he had had no plans to break up and he too had always wondered why I had broken up with him. The moral is to check things out before you act!

Our freshman year, the student body president (grandpa-who else?) came up with a sinister plan to raise money for a popcorn machine in the gym. He would auction the underclass students to the seniors as slaves for a lunch hour of servitude.

Jeannie and I volunteered to be slaves and we were bought by a group of senior boys who had pooled their money. To our delight, they had nothing planned for us to do but instead let us loiter on the sacred Senior Lawn with them. Each class had a designated lawn, but the Senior Lawn was the most prominent and the most sacred.

When grandpa came by and saw us on his blessed Senior Lawn, he immediately demanded to know what authority we had to be there. When one of the boys confessed that we were purchased, but they had no job for us, that cheapskate suggested we wash his car. We did, but complained the entire time about anyone who was too cheap to buy a slave and then would borrow someone else's. I certainly didn't have him on my get to know better list!

I am always surprised when I see a low student turnout at a high school sport event. Often in these days there are more parents than kids in attendance. Maybe we just had fewer distractions in our day, but when a basketball game was going, and we weren't working, we were there.

That brings me to the legendary basketball tournament of 1953. It was the final game of the tournament. We were playing Simi and the winner would win the championship. The score was tied and just as the bell rang your grandpa shot a basket at half court. We won! The crowd went wild with joy. Hmmm, I thought, "maybe he did have some good qualities after all."

Sometime about the end of the year, we were called in for a school assembly. Since we only had about 350 in our high school and another 200 in junior high, it was easy to have assemblies. We even had assemblies on such things as hygiene (sponsored by Lux soap) and hair care (sponsored by Toni home permanents).

Assemblies were always a welcome relief from Spanish with Mr. O'Neil anyway, so I was happy to go. This time the assembly was actually an inauguration of new student body officers and there was Mr. Tommy Russell handing over the gavel to his successor.

However, before he did so, he decided to thank us all as a student body for all the help he had received to make the year a success. (He forgot to mention his free car wash). Then he began to thank God for how his life had been changed when he turned it over to him. I was astonished. What courage he had to share his faith before the entire student body. I felt a new respect for him then. My conscience was pricked. Maybe my faith had not grown because I had been so reticent about sharing it. For that glimpse of the bravery grandpa had at that time, and for how it changed my perspective of him, I AM GLAD

Mark 8:38 For whoever is ashamed of Me and My words ion this adulterous and sinful generation, of him the Son Of Man also will be ashamed when He comes in the glory of His Father with the holy angels.

2ndTimothy 1:12b I am not ashamed, for I know whom I have believed and am persuaded that He is able to keep what I have committed to Him until that Day.

No wonder Revelations speaks of the fact that cowards will not be in Heaven. I was a coward. Do you speak up for what you believe? Ask God to help you be braver and then Just Do It!

New Horizons

I was a sophomore in high school when my perspectives changed. One day I was walking down the hall when Mr. Roller, one of our teachers, stepped out of his room and yelled at me, "Miss McCay, get in here." I was stunned. What in the world had I done?

It turns out that Mr. Roller headed up a group called The California Scholarship Society. I had heard of it but had no idea what it was about. Well, this club is based on academic achievement and in our school, at that time, you were automatically in if your grades met a certain criteria. I was in.

I wasn't in many clubs. I worked a lot and at that time I had a babysitting job that meant I walked from school and across Ojai after school every day to take care of a little guy while his mom worked evenings for her mother in a little downtown restaurant named Norma's. My mom worked days there as a cook so we had a connection.

I made $15.00 a week. The baby's mom usually got home much later than her scheduled 9:00. Apparently, her stress relief was a trip by the bar located nearby. Luckily, I have always been a night owl anyway, so I wasn't usually sleep deprived and I liked the freedom that the money gave me while my bank account grew. It took a serious dent in my social life though.

I didn't get to go to my Scholarship Society welcome party due to work, but this group provided a lot of incentive for me to stay on track. With dad coughing up $5.00 for every straight A semester report card and the pride of belonging to this club, I stayed on for my entire high school experience. I was encouraged to go to college, which had never occurred to me. I was exposed to different values and goals. I was an elected officer in the club. I liked the feeling of belonging and especially helping to plan the activities. I am very thankful for Mr. Roller who sought me out and welcomed me in.

Years later, in working for Social Services, I wondered how many kids are over looked, who just need a little encouragement or a sense of belonging to stay on course.

I had the Meiners Oak's gang over whenever possible. Since the Whitney's had left, the little apartment in the back was usually vacant so I had a few small slumber parties there, but when it was just Jeanne, we stayed in my room while my loyal sweet sister volunteered to sleep in our closet, so we could have the bed. One night when we were in a deep discussion about the merits of certain boys (what else), I heard a muffled snicker. Little Janice was enjoying the whole conversation. No wonder she was so willing to give up her side of the bed.

Dating in our day, meant the boy came to the house, walked to the door, introduced himself, got the family approval and set a time to be home. In my house it also meant that when the boy walked me to the door after a date, the venation blinds would begin to part in various places, while my curious siblings assessed the situation. How unnerving is that?

Now our front porch extended across most of the front of our house with exception of my parents' bedroom. One night I returned home from a date, and in addition to the usual venation blind activity, there was a weeping and crying coming out of the open window of my parents' bedroom. My mother was praying for all of us in earnest. She was especially praying for me. Well, that was a bummer and sooo embarrassing. How was I going to explain that? I didn't have too. He never ask me out again,

How foolish and prideful I so often was! My parents believed in God and they prayed. How many parents do take the time to earnestly pray for their children? They wanted the best for me. Maybe, I was feeling guilty too. I was doubting the very faith I had been taught to believe in.

Whenever possible, Jeanne and I liked to double date. We always took along that little brownie camera I had received as a gift so many years ago. We had plenty of evidence of some great times and if the dates turned out to be duds, we had fun anyway.

One fun Sunday afternoon we went boating in Carpentaria with George Skelton and Ron Johnson and possibly George's brother Chaz. The boat leaked and I suspect they might have needed a couple more balers, hence the invite. I was panicked, but I was glad to have a mom praying for me that day, because I would have sank if the boat sank. I still could not swim.

Ojai was never exactly the Bible belt for evangelicals. Evangelicals, are people who believe the Bible is the inspired word of God, salvation is a personal and individual decision, and the afterlife is just as Jesus talked about in the Gospel's. There will be an eternal life in Heaven for Believers and those who are not will be eternally separated from God.

Ojai seemed to have a lot of diverse religions, or supposed paths to God, which some assumed to be more enlightened. As I was exposed to more of this, I had plenty of questions. Was this possible? Were we too narrow minded? What about all the hypocrites I had met along the way? Where were they going?

The church we attended, Oak View Full Gospel, took a very literal view of the Bible. We "shunned" behavior that would lead away from a lifestyle that the Bible taught was right. We did not drink because it could lead to drunkenness which the Bible condemned. Smoking was forbidden because it would destroy the wonderful body God had put us in; there was no couples dancing because it could lead to temptation and sex outside of marriage is not God's perfect plan. Any entertainment that glorified bad behavior was not approved.

In addition, women were to dress modestly. In fact, once when our dear pastor showed up unexpectedly and saw me wearing a pair of my beloved shorts, he managed to work that into his Sunday sermon. He didn't exactly mention my name, but mom and I both knew who he was speaking about.

Of course, I thought the church was just too confining about some of its tenets. While, I never saw any reason to drink alcohol and smoking always seemed like a great waste of hard earned money I was not willing to give in on the dancing issue. So, after one semester of sitting out the dance lessons Mrs. Glover taught in gym on Friday's, I conveniently decided to forego that part of the church's teaching by reasoning that I was not a member of the church anyway. I deserted sweet Beverly and joined the dancers.

Years later, after Grandpa and I were married, we were at a function where people were having fun dancing and then we noticed some very flirtatious behavior between married people and people who were not married to each other. Only then did it sink in why the Oak View Church had put that as part of their recommendations.

Marriage is very sacred and we should protect it above every other relationship. We could always put on a record and dance at home with each other anyway, so we eventually joined a church a lot like the church I had grown up in.

The funny thing about our little Oak View church is that it was growing and there was a wonderful feeling of love there. These self-sacrificing people genuinely cared about us, about each other and about the commission to reach a lost world. I could not deny that.

Meanwhile, thanks to the Scholarship Society, Mr. Roller took us on a trip to U.C.L.A. I had never been on a university campus. I was in awe of everything. There was such a respect for education. College was within my reach. I knew my parents would support whatever I chose.

With my new found vision, I began to feel quite mature. One Saturday, I decided to get rid of some stuff from my past life and tossed a bunch of unneeded things in the trash. Then I decided to surprise mom again with a clean house, when she got home from work. I would need to organize my reluctant brothers.

One, in particular, was busy reading something he was enjoying so immensely that he kept laughing out loud. It made me smile just to think of how much enjoyment he was getting. I decided to sneak around and see what it was. Can you believe it? He was reading my old diary which he had retrieved from the trash! Now I have promised your great Uncle Keith I would stop telling "Keith stories" so I will not divulge what one of your dear great uncles is lucky to be alive today.

Over the years I have grown to appreciate the Oak View Church. I wasn't its best product, but the values taught there kept me from a lot of mischief and for that I AM GLAD

Proverbs 3:5-7 Trust in the Lord with all your heart, and do not lean on your own understanding. In all your ways acknowledge him, and he will make straight your paths. Be not wise in your own eyes: fear the Lord, and turn away from evil.

How often we come as close the edge of life's cliff's as we can and then are surprised when we fall off. Don't take that risk !

Sixteen at Last

I was barely sixteen when I began to receive strange letters in the mail almost daily. Each letter purported to be from a boy named Eddie, who I had never met. The letters proclaimed my incredible beauty and how desperate was this young man's love for me. Hmm —-was I being stalked by some mad man or had someone finally noticed me for what I hoped I was. Maybe sitting with my elbows in lemon peels to bleach them out, or my faithfully used supply of White Rain Crème Rinse promising to bring out the highlights in my mousy brown hair was finally paying off.

After a while, I began to receive phone calls from my mystery man. It turns out that he attended a local private boy's school named Villanova. At that time there were many young men from Central and South America who attended the school. Apparently, the isolation from young ladies of similar age had driven some to desperation, or maybe it was simply the Latin blood.

After numerous phone calls, it was decided that I would attend a Villanova function that would be well chaperoned. So much so, that I would need to get my own ride there and back! Finally I managed to convince mom that it just had to be safe and I was so curious to meet this young man. Also, several girls I knew had boyfriends there, so I would not be alone if everything turned out to be a disaster

It turns out that Eddie was actually the student body president, a good athlete, and an excellent student. He never admitted where he had first seen me. (Maybe he hadn't?) Later I found out that some of the phrases he had used in his proclamation of my astounding beauty and his profound attraction to me, had actually come from a book he had purchased. How tacky is that!

There was, from the beginning, no future in any relationship but it made for a perfect set up that year. He was from a wealthy family in Mexico and had received his early education in England so he could do a very good English accent and had an excellent vocabulary. He had also been exposed to so much of the world that I had not, so it was intriguing to listen to him. Dating opportunities were limited. (Dating a boy in a private school may be somewhat akin to dating a prisoner).

That Christmas, I came down with a terrible case of the measles and my entire vacation was spent in bed. (That was before we could be immunized for the measles). Now I had a very big date with Eddie the first weekend in January. There was some kind of a big shindig in Santa Barbara for promising young men from the Catholic schools. A priest from Villanova would be taking several couples over. I had purchased a beautiful pink chiffon dress at Jack Rose for this ominous occasion.

As the time for the event grew close, I proclaimed myself well. The measles were almost gone and I was out of the contagious stage. Yes, I still felt weak, but I had the willpower to overcome this (didn't I). Besides, hadn't I told all my close friends I was going?

As soon as we arrived at the beautiful hotel where the dinner was taking place, I felt more like throwing up than eating. I began to have chills. People seemed to be avoiding me. I went to the ladies room and discovered that I was covered with bright red measles. I was in major relapse.

Going home, the priest suggested I sit up in front to keep from contaminating the others. Another disaster to chalk up to life's experiences, not to mention my pride.

My mostly phone and letter romance ended when he went off the college the following year and I went on to my senior year in high school. He was decent and honorable and there were no regrets. We had nothing in common, but thanks to his connections, I had met some very interesting people and had an expanded world view. I recommend expanding your horizons as long as you do not forget who you are and what you believe.

My pride took another hit that year. Our cousin, Florence Anderson, who had grown up in Bismarck was both talented and beautiful. She left for New York soon after the war and renamed herself the stage name of Lynn Dollar. After that, she secured a position as the beautiful assistant on the most popular game show going, The $64,000 Question.

Though, I had little contact with her, she was still family so I liked to let everyone know that we were related. No one believed me until a scandal broke out on the show. Somehow, some contestant was being fed the answers and a disgruntled whistle blower exposed it all. The show went off the air in shame. Now suddenly everyone remembered I was related. So much for the popular sport of name dropping.

Mr. Thompson's Biology class delved into the basic forms of life and how amazing we are created, Of course, he believed in evolution and I could not swallow that. How could a piece of slime eventually produce something as complex as an eye, which is still not understood by scientists? When did the slime begin to think?

All this made me all the more convinced that only God could have created us. If God had created us, wouldn't He have had a plan and a purpose for us? I had to discount any recent religions that had arrived on the scene because that would have to mean all the people before that, would have had no chance to know God. Surely that could not have been his plan.

By this time, thanks to many hours in church, I had a pretty good understanding of what Judeo-Christian meant. The Old Testament goes back to the beginning of creation and how man decided not to obey God and instead followed Satan, who was a beautiful angel who had been kicked out of heaven when he tried to usurp God. As soon as the disobedience happened, evil entered into man's heart, but God promised that he would provide a way back to him one day. Meanwhile, God set in place rules for men to follow such as the 10 commandments.

That made sense to me. I had seen evil. I remembered the war and we were just beginning to understand how evil man's heart can get. There were still people in the world who were intent on destroying us, and who imprisoned people who believed in God. There is a lot of evil in this world. It does not come from God. It comes from the absence of God. Where there is a void, Satan will surely fill it.

Now all my thinking was beginning to cause a problem for me. If God had a purpose for me, hadn't I better find out what it was? If I allowed a void in my life, would it eventually be filled with evil or at least, a lifestyle that would lead away from him? If I truly surrendered my life to God, what would I have to give up?

When I took Chemistry from Mr. Thompson the following year, I managed to have a minor explosion in class with a silly little experiment on evaporation. His comment to me was, "Miss McCay, sit down and think, think, think!" Well, I must say it was really his biology class that had started the whole thinking process.

My Junior year of high school ended with a whole lot of questions about my future and about my life. For all the prayers on my behalf and all the examples I had to help me eventually sort things out, I AM GLAD.

Psalms 53:1a The fool has said in his heart, "there is no God". (NKJ)

What do you think happens to fools who do not believe in God?

Checking my Wounds for Pride

At the beginning of the summer, Janice Cornine and I took a trip to San Francisco to visit some of her family's friends, the Haglers. The cost of the train was $16.00 and it was a small price to pay for such a taste of freedom. Of course, we were under somewhat of the watchful eye of her parent's friends, but they seemed to let us plan our days anyway we liked. What an adventure we had as we scurried around San Francisco by trolley and bus. Our horizons were expanding again.

Meanwhile, dad was diligently looking for just the right car for me. I had that expanding bank account and I had passed my driving test. What other criteria could there be?

When I got home dad told me about a car he had found. It sounded just like what I needed or was that wanted? It was 1941 light blue Buick convertible with new seat covers, a new top, and white sidewall tires. My dreams had come true. I could hardly wait to show it off.

The first day of my Senior year in high school I proudly drove my new dream car up to the parking lot only to discover that there was a light blue Chevy convertible, the exact same shade of blue as mine, already parked there. It turns out that another girl named Cynthia had the same taste in cars as I did, and to top it off, she was a year younger. Another lesson in pride!

As I dutifully took my place in band that year, Mr Kaiser assigned me to first chair, first place clarinet. Now I know this was more of a reward for showing up the last 5 years for band, then for any perceived talent. I never took my clarinet home to practice, but nevertheless, I was happy for the honor. Alas, however, another new boy had joined the band the year before. His name was James Norton and he really wanted that position. In fact, he had attempted to dazzle the band teacher, Mr. Kaiser, the year before with trilling in some extra notes for some of our pieces .Mr. Kaiser was not impressed.

Actually, since our band was the last period of the day for the entire 6 years, I always suspected Mr. Kaiser had a full blown headache by then, anyway. I had no doubt that James took the clarinet a whole lot more seriously than I did and probably deserved the position on merit. Nonetheless I had every intention of keeping it. After all, both of us were playing 1st clarinet music no matter if we sat in the 1st or 2nd chair, of the 1st clarinet position.

Now our band practiced on the stage of the auditorium and every day we dragged our own chairs and music stands out to set up before we began our practice session. My seventh period class, just preceding band, was gym on the exact opposite end of the campus. About the 3rd day of our chair assignment, I arrived to find that James had positioned his chair so close to the end of the stage, that he had stolen my position. Mr. Kaiser did not notice. The next day, I made sure I could shower quickly and make it across campus to put my chair in it's rightful place. James still managed to squeeze his chair in so close it is a wonder he didn't fall off the stage. Mr. Kaiser still did not notice which proved my headache theory.

The race was on. Every day I cut gym as short as possible. No chit chat for me. I was on a mission. I put my chair so far to the end of the stage that James could not get his in. I was probably getting more exercise sprinting across campus than in gym.

One day the gym teacher, Mrs. Johnson, delayed me with some idle chatter. She asked what my hurry always was. How could I possibly explain how petty I was being? Petty, that's what it was for sure. When I realized how silly the whole thing had gotten, I made a major decision to let it go. James could have the spot. Besides I was missing the chit-chat anyway. You know how grandma loves to talk!

Somehow, pride can rob us of the things we enjoy most. Was my car any less lovely because someone else had a similar one? Was the sound emitted by the band any less tuneful because I had to sit in a different chair? Who knows what pressure James was in to perform?

From those lessons I have since tried to check myself when I feel disappointed or wounded about something, and determine if the only thing hurting is my pride and I AM GLAD.

Almost all, if not all of the hurts we have can be traced back to pride. We think we deserved better treatment. We think our life status should be better. We think we are the one who should have had the promotion or the raise or the nicest, richest, best looking spouse or date.

The Bible has so much to say about Pride. For instance, Proverbs 13:10 says it is what causes strife and Proverbs 29:23 says it is what brings a man low. Whenever you are in a dismal situation and feeling sorry for yourself, check and see if the only thing that has been hurt is your pride. If so, just realize that only when we are humbled can we grow to be what God intended.

James 4:10 'Humble yourself in the sight of the Lord, and He will lift you up. (NKV)

Then Came Grandpa Tom

We had one telephone located in a central hall. With six kids there were plenty of calls and plenty of messages that never got communicated to the proposed recipient.

Important calls were the ones related to jobs. Though my dad had always proclaimed that we weren't poor—we just didn't have any money. We, kids, had long ago decided that not having money was pretty close to being poor. Job opportunities were not to be missed. Social calls were another matter. They could always call back.

One day my brother Keith was relating the athletic prowess of a boy named Russell. Mom ask if that was the boy who kept calling for Gladys. This was news to me. I knew it wasn't your great uncle Nelson Russell, because he was younger and had a beautiful girlfriend.

A few days later, I did happen to answer the phone when a very nervous young man named Tom very curtly ask if I wanted to go out to a ballgame Friday night. The wheels in my head were turning. I knew 3 Toms? Then it occurred to me that maybe the Russell boy was Nelson's older brother, the cheapskate who had had me wash his car when I was a lowly freshmen.

I also remembered his testimony in the last school assembly. I decided that it would be worth getting to know him and I said yes. He said he would pick me up at 6 and hung up before I could get any other information. Now I began to wonder what Tom it was. I worried that it might not be the right one, and then I wondered what I would do. Perhaps I could feign a sudden case of the intentional flu?

Friday night came and, of course, I was just a bit late, but no Tom had arrived. Well, that did it. It probably was that Tommy Russell and I decided to revert back to my original opinion of him. My brothers and friends were busy, as usual, playing basketball on the sport court when I heard someone call out, "Tom". I checked and sure enough. They had told your Grandpa Tom, I was late. Why waste time? They had invited him to play basketball, while I finished getting ready!

Our very first date was January 24^{th1}. I remember because it was my brother Loring's birthday. A birthday celebration at the McCay's usually consisted of a birthday cake at dinner and a "pinch" to "grow and inch" so I was free to go after this momentous occasion.

I was wearing a pink sweater and a white skirt. Grandpa looked pretty cute in his plaid shirt, but with the sweat dripping off of his forehead, I sure hoped he had one of those powerful deodorants working for him. (He did).

Grandpa had a 1952 tan Mercury. What a conservative young man he was! We went to a Ventura College basketball game.

Afterward he decided to take me out to a place that made pizzas. It was the only place in Ventura that made them and it was a whole new concept in our area. I had never had a pizza. I had never even heard of Pizza

He ordered Pizza and then decided to use the Gentlemen's facility. The waiter asked what I would like and I didn't know what to say so I did the polite thing. I ordered the same and congratulated myself on my good manners.

Guess what? We got 2 huge Pizzas and poor grandpa only had the money for one. I had no idea a pizza was something you could share. Luckily, I had enough money to pay for my own pizza. We certainly weren't getting off to a good start.

Grandpa was very interested in what I believed. That following Sunday he ask if he could go to church with me. I should have told him to eat a big breakfast, our services could go on for quite a while.

Sure enough, we had an unusually anointed service. By 1:p.m. his stomach was growling so loudly that it gave me the giggles. One look from Brother Mac and I was cured. The service lasted until 1:30. Grandpa Tom suggested we visit his church the next Sunday.

By our 3rd date your grandpa was asking how many children I wanted. I thought that was a little nosey. He said he wanted two. I said that would be far too boring. We had a family of six kids and a variety of others who seemed to get dropped off at our place from time to time. In fact, mom and dad soon added two other real McCays but I had no idea that was going to happen at that time. I wanted no less than six kids, so obviously gramps was not in my future.

Grandpa always amazed me. He knew every verse from every song in the song book at church. He had a lot of scripture memorized. He had very definite ideas about everything. His father struggled with alcohol, but grandpa Tom had never had a drink, even when he was in a fraternity at Berkeley. He had strong convictions about many things.

Grandpa Tom began to tell me that he was praying for a wife and he felt I was the one God wanted him to marry. Doesn't that sound like a good line? I wasn't so sure where the message was coming from. Besides, I wanted a big family like I had grown up in. He decided he was willing to compromise on four. (For good measure we actually were blest with 5)

Our dating consisted mostly of going to every kind of game in the county, attending church (usually mine), and attending a few formals. In addition Grandpa Tom played on a semi pro baseball team, helped coach our high school baseball team and was a very competitive county-wide badminton player.

After a few months, we were definitely going steady. I had accumulated his much decorated Letterman's sweater and a bevy of other items such as class ring etc. that symbolized our relationship.

During this time, Grandpa Tom had been nominated for the Air Force academy by local congressman Teague. He left with several other guys to test for this, and when he was gone he sent me a postcard indicating that he and 3 other guys had gone out the night before with 4 girls. What a creep!!

I packed up all of his items and when he arrived home and came to see me, I simply opened the door and threw everything out at him. He kept knocking to ask what was wrong. I went to get the offending card and then noticed that my fun loving dad was the one who had added, "with 4 girls." I was so embarrassed. Dad hadn't even used the same color pen. I guess I hadn't learned much from my first breakup as a freshmen, after all.

One day I was being picked up after school by my mom to take a trip to Ventura. I had ridden the bus to school that day. When I got to the car I found that Tommy had picked a bunch of roses from his aunts yard (hopefully with permission) and had been waiting for me when he spotted my mom's car and learned that she was picking me up, He left the roses with mom.

Never one to waste time, he was busy playing handball when I got out of school. Looking a whole lot like I had seen him that very first date out playing basketball with my brothers, I remember very definitely feeling my heart skip a beat. I was 17. Was this love? You guessed it. Even today, grandpa makes my heart skip a beat when I hear his voice or when I spot him somewhere in a crowd.

Our pastor, brother Mac, loved Tom. Pastor Mac also shared his great affection for baseball, and besides, he was worried that I would go off to the University at Berkeley and become a Communist. Berkeley was known to produce some real radicals, even back then. Maybe this would change my mind. I think Brother Mac thought Tommy was an answer to his prayers too

Now you know that this family believes in education. Your mom and your aunts all went to college. I began going to community college that summer and continued college for many years. The question really was whether or not Berkeley was right for me then.

Grandpa Tom had spent a year at Berkeley and came home broke and sick the summer after his freshmen year. He finished 2 years at Ventura Junior College and debated going back to Berkeley but really wanted more to get a good engineering job and get on with his life.

Engineers were in demand back in the mid 1950's .Our country was growing. We were in a baby boom. Grandpa Tom took a test to go to work for the California Engineering Department and he passed it in May of 1956.

In the midst of all this, grandpa attended my senior functions with me. I had made several new close friends and one was Dora Brown, a sweet quiet young lady who lived in the Arbolada. I thought it would be nice to have a senior party at her house. She was dubious. Her mother thought it was a grand idea. Since Dora had no idea of my previous luck with parties, she finally went along with it.

The party was a dress up affair, and we had it the last week of school. All I really remember is that Bill Smith, our senior class president, turned up in a cutoff tuxedo and grandpa, spent most of the evening talking baseball strategy with Dave Cook and other members of our high school baseball team. Mrs. Brown thought it a great success, but I rather think it was less than memorable.

With the assurance that he would be embarking on a real career, Grandpa Tom presented me with an engagement ring. The night he asked me to marry him, he sang two songs to me: Tell Me Why and With These Hands I'll Provide For You.

I went home to show mom and dad my ring. Mom was flabbergasted. She said, "You can't get married—I am pregnant" That's when I learned that there as going to be another addition to the McCay tribe. Mom was 4 months pregnant. She thought it would look funny for her to be in a maternity dress at my wedding. Little Mark was due in October.

The following week I applied for a job at Bank of America. I got the job and was told I could start to work the very week after I graduated. We had already decided we would need to get married either very soon or after the new little McCay arrived. We decided on very soon, and set the date for July 14th.

People did not play married or move in with each other to decide if a person was a good fit back then, and for good reason.

Marriage is a very sacred thing. The Bible tells us that when two people get married they are united as one. (And by the way, we are talking about marriage between the opposite sex here.)

As I was busy learning a new job at the bank and grandpa Tom was busy learning to become a surveyor on Conejo grade, Mom was busy with my wedding. She bought loads of yellow dotted swiss and made bridesmaid dresses for Janice Cornine, Dora Brown, my sister Janice, and my singer, a high school friend named Sharon Hill. Mom ordered invitations. flowers and a wedding cake. I was clueless as to how to plan a wedding and I am sure mom was too, but she really wanted me to have a nice one.

We went to Jack Rose to find the perfect wedding dress. It cost over $100.00 and was featured on the cover of Modern Bride in June that year. This was an amazing sacrifice on the part of mom and dad and I am forever grateful.

We had two counseling sessions with Pastor Mac. That should be enough. After all, at age 17 and age 20, we thought we probably knew just about everything! (He did suggest that we not kiss until we were married—he was a little late on that one!)

My mom gave me two pieces of advice for marriage. She said that whenever possible, I should always go where my husband went. That is why your mom's spent so much time under the bleachers at ballgames. Grandpa loved to play ball and he was always involved in sports as a high school referee or with a team. The other advice was that no matter how big of a disagreement we had, we should never stop being affectionate to each other. That advice would save a lot of marriages!

We were the first couple to marry in the new Oak View Full Gospel Lighthouse Church. The reception was held in the yard of some friends of mom and dad who happened to live next door to the church. Grandpa Tom's baseball manager was at our wedding and he wondered if Tom could possible make it back for the scheduled baseball game the next day. We nixed that, but it might have been a good idea since we actually had almost no money.

We had both been on our new jobs only about six weeks, and due to the lack of computers in those days, we were still not processed to get paid. The little money we had had was needed to rent a cottage, help some on the wedding, and set up housekeeping.

Grandpa Tom has always been the emotional one. While I was walking down the aisle, the little 3 year old boy who was living with mom and dad, saw Grandpa Tommy's tears and at a very quiet moment he said, "why is Tommy crying? Doesn't he want to marry Gladys?" That certainly broke the tension!

I remember thinking that no matter what, I was making a promise to God when I married grandpa, and I would do every-thing I could to make this marriage work.

Our honeymoon consisted of a trip to Knott's Berry Farm, Sunday morning church, an LA Angels game (before they became professional) and home to our tiny apartment.

Grandpa Tom had both Monday and Tuesday off for the honeymoon, but he used Tuesday to go up to the country club and caddy for some quick cash so we could eat. Neither of was willing to mention our financial plight to anyone. That was a few years before Visa or Master card so when you had no money, you were actually broke.

We charged our gas at a friend's filling station and I finally got a $40.00 advance at work. Meanwhile, the Oak View church gave us a pantry shower. (Somebody must have figured out our plight.) We received a very interesting assortment of pantry items and decided that maybe some people were using the opportunity to clean out their own pantries. Believe me though, we were happy to have those items and since this was long before cans were dated, I can assure you that expired food will not (usually) kill you. (Just be sure it hasn't changed its consistency, color or smell.)

Grandpa Tom has always had a lot of side jobs to augment his income and to support our family. Never have too much pride to work! As long as you are healthy and strong you will be able to find something to do and each job will give you experience for a better job.

When Grandpa Tom and I were married we decided that we would always have one date night a week. However, this became a little complicated when we had three toddlers and I was going to college at night. Grandpa decided that we would get a babysitter for one night and he would take classes with me and that would also be our date.

We took a Sociology class together and one day we took a test on compatibility. Of all the people in the class, we were the most opposite. Doesn't that tell you that people who decide to leave a marriage because they have nothing in common are using a lame excuse?

We have been blest beyond belief in 58 years of marriage. We have built 2 homes, acquired 5 wonderful son in laws, added 14 amazing grandchildren and 5 adorable great grandchildren.

We were not perfect parents (you may have heard this rumor) and we have been through some rocky spots, but we have learned an astounding secret to marriage and to happiness. When we put God as our priority and our focus, everything else so marvelously falls into place.

For the wonderful family God put me in, for the joy of a husband and children who love the Lord, and for all the blessings I have been provided I AM GLAD

Proverbs 3: 5&6 Trust in the Lord with all you heart, and lean not on your own understanding; in all your ways acknowledge Him, and he shall direct your paths. (NKJ)

Jeremiah 9:23 Let not the wise man glory in his wisdom, Let not the mighty man glory in his might, Nor the rich man glory in his riches,

But let him who glories glory in this,
That he understands and knows Me,
For I am the Lord, exercising
Loving-kindness, judgment, and
Righteousness in the earth
For in these I delight, says the Lord. (NKJ)

Beloved grandchildren (and anyone else who may happen upon this book), please know that we are always ready to share your problems and to pray with you. Grandpa and I are just a phone call away.

the end

Photos

❈

50 Years

The McCay family a few months before leaving North Dakota

One of those summer vacations

Family Ties

That infamous corduroy Suit

McCay Roots

Future weight watchers Candidate

That 1946 Chevy and green trailer

Fit for a family of 8

6

Side view of our Washington Mansion

Precious Memories

Jeannie and me

At 15

Basking on George Skelton's boat

In that stolen bathing suit!

Our
Growing
Family

50 Years

Love   Love   Love

CPSIA information can be obtained
at www.ICGtesting.com
Printed in the USA
FSOW04n2144040615
7675FS